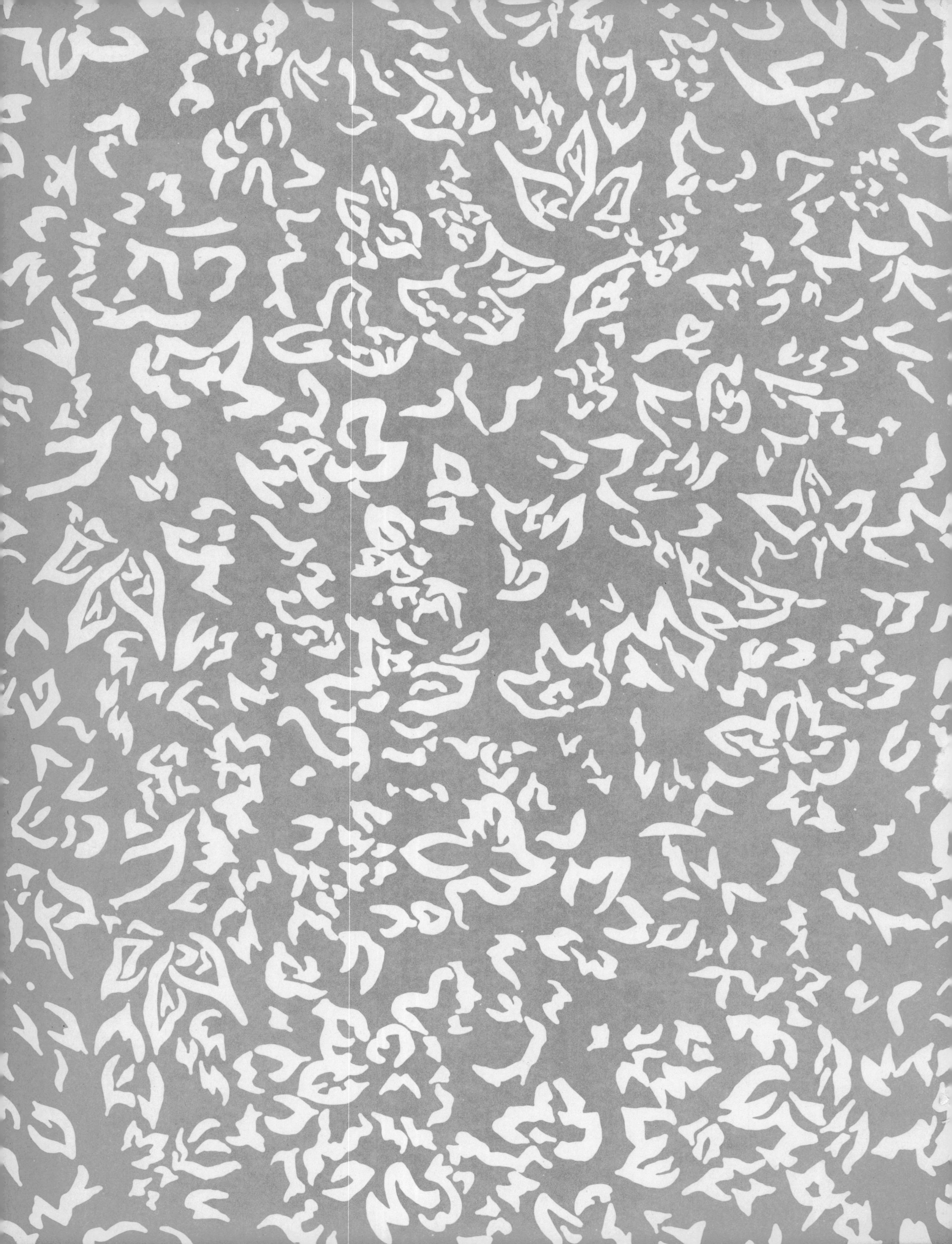

Mary Cassatt

A Private World

Mary Cassatt

A Private World

ILLUSTRATIONS FROM THE
NATIONAL GALLERY OF ART

MARA R. WITZLING

UNIVERSE

Published in the United States of America in 1991
by UNIVERSE
300 Park Avenue South, New York, NY 10010

ISBN: 0-87663-616-4

Library of Congress Catalog Card Number:
91-31698

91 92 93 94 95 / 10 9 8 7 6 5 4 3 2 1

Printed in Hong Kong

TABLE OF CONTENTS

Mary Cassatt
A Private World

Mara R. Witzling

An American expatriate whose entire career was spent in France, Mary Cassatt's name is now familiar to the general public and her work is accepted within the art historical canon (although as recently as 1973, a major history of Impressionism included only a brief discussion of her work.[1]) Unlike other American painters whose work transposed some aspects of the Impressionist style to an American context, Cassatt was the only American artist who was closely affiliated with the French Impressionists and she participated in four of their exhibitions between 1879 and 1886. She was instrumental in bringing Impressionism to the attention of the American public through her advice to major collectors, particularly Louisine and H. O. Havemeyer. Cassatt's decision to remain in France—where she found greater personal and artistic freedom than in her native country—proved vital to the success of her career, as had Harriet Hosmer's move to Rome and John Singer Sargent's settling in London. Cassatt's tenacious professionalism in the forefront of the public arena gave evidence of a career pattern that could be described as masculine. Yet her choice of subjects and its emphasis on domestic, particularly maternal, themes represented a world view that is traditionally perceived as feminine. Cassatt's Impressionist work exhibited formal innovation and skill at recording the spontaneous gesture. Her choosing to combine a professional approach to her artistic career and an emphasis on recording the ephemeral activities of the domestic sphere contributed to the acceptance of domestic interactions as serious artistic subject matter.

Cassatt's first exposure to European culture occurred during her childhood. One of her earliest childhood memories, as recounted to her biographer Achille Segard, was of learning to read in Paris as a little girl. She came from a privileged background—her mother belonged to an old Pennsylvania family, her father was a stockbrocker—although the family's frequent changes of residence could be viewed as somewhat unconventional. They moved within Pennsylvania at first, but in 1851 left for Europe, stopping briefly in Paris before continuing on to Darmstadt, Germany, to find treatment for Cassatt's brother Robert's knee joint disease and to allow another brother, Alexander, to study engineering. Robert died in 1855, and the Cassatts remained abroad until 1858 when they finally returned to Pennsylvania. In 1860, upon turning sixteen, Cassatt enrolled in the Pennsylvania Academy of the Fine Arts where she studied for the next five years, progressing from drawing from the models of antiquity through life drawing to painting. The women's curriculum differed at that time from the men's only in its omission of study from the nude model. All accounts suggest that Cassatt was part of a lively and committed group of young artists who were dedicated to becoming professionals. She found a special friend at the Academy in Eliza Haldeman, with whose brother Carsten she carried on a mild flirtation.

As early as 1860, just at the time she decided to become a painter, Cassatt realized she would need at some point to continue her studies abroad. That same year, her brother Alexander wrote, "In three years Mary will want to go to Rome to study."[2] Not quite according to his predictions, Cassatt left for Paris late in 1865 and never again lived in the United States, with the exception of a short period of exile (1870–71) forced by the Franco-Prussian War. During the next fifty-five years, she made only three other trips back "home," allegedly because acute seasickness prevented more voyages. Her expatriation contributed to her achievement of a professional status that was far superior to that which she could have attained had she remained in the United States. Evidence of this came, for example, during her penultimate stateside visit in 1898, when a newspaper notice identified Cassatt not as a recognized artist, but as a sister of the Pennsylvania Railroad president, and mentioned the exceptionally small size of her dog, but nothing about her own distinguished reputation.[3]

Cassatt's decision to remain abroad represented a response to at least three factors. First, during the nineteenth century, many American artists suffered from a cultural inferiority complex. Cassatt was not alone in considering Europe, the Old World, the source of art and culture. A "grand tour" had become a necessary part of any cultured person's—and particularly any artist's—education, and several American artists of both genders extended this to pursue their careers abroad. Then, too, Cassatt having defined herself as a professional woman artist, found more opportunity and acceptance in a European art center than in Victorian-era America. As she remarked in 1894, "Above all give me France—women do not have to fight for recognition here, if they do serious work."[4] (Slightly earlier in the century, for similar reasons, the American sculptor Harriet Hosmer had immigrated to Rome, where she was later followed by a group later

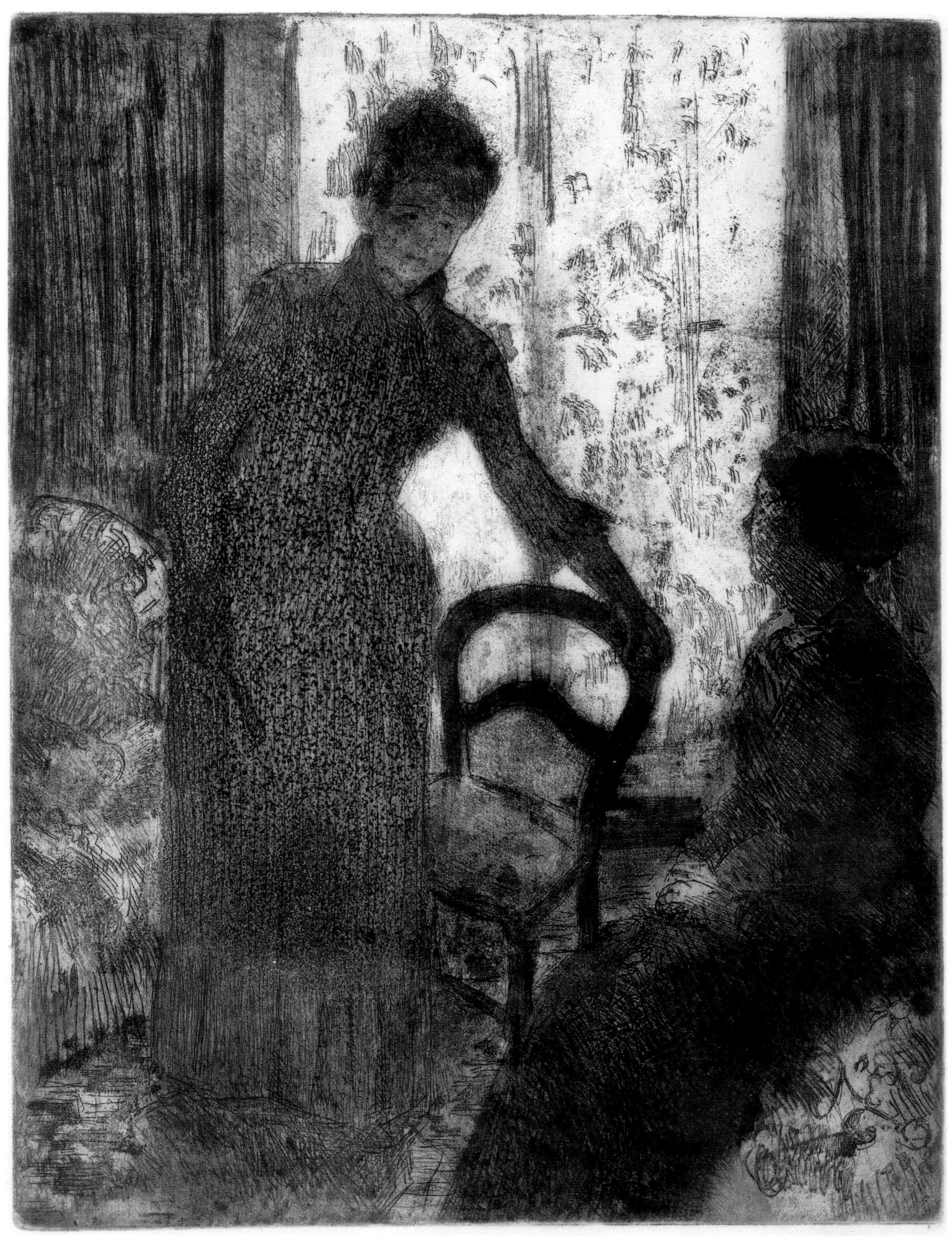

The Visitor (Breeskin 34 v/vi), c. 1880
Soft-ground etching, aquatint, and drypoint
0.397 × 0.310 m (15⅝ × 12 $^{11}/_{16}$ in.)
Rosenwald Collection 1946.21.94

described by Henry James as a "white marmorean flock"—approximately five other American women sculptors who were also expatriates.) Finally, the modernist idiom that she espoused made it especially important for Cassatt to remain abroad. In Paris, she was exposed to and ultimately became an integral part of an artistic avant-garde that was nonexistent in the United States.

Cassatt's first decade abroad was a period of apprenticeship in which she traveled frequently, exposing herself to diverse artistic influences, including some formal instruction. Because, as a woman, she was prohibited from attending classes at the École des Beaux-Arts when she first arrived in Paris, she took private lessons from Jean-Léon Gérôme. With Eliza Haldeman, she traveled to Écouen in the countryside outside Paris, and participated in an art colony led by two genre painters, Pierre Édouard Frère and Paul Soyer. In 1868, she studied with Thomas Couture near Écouen and in 1870, with Charles Bellay in Rome. The tight structure and substantial figures of her mature works show the legacy of these teachers. By the time of her 1870 return to the United States, her style had already begun to mature: two of her four submissions had been accepted by the Paris Salon, *Mandolin Player* in 1868 (under the name of Mary Stevenson) and *A Peasant Woman from Fabello, Sesia Valley (Piémont)* in 1870.

In the fall of 1870, the outbreak of the Franco-Prussian war forced Cassatt to return to the United States where she remained, without enthusiasm, until December 1871. Her letters to her friend Emily Sartain (an engraver from a prominent Philadelphia family of artists, including her father, John Sartain) show how unhappy Cassatt was in the States and how she ached to return to Europe, hoping especially to go to Spain, which she fantasized as an artist's haven. "I have been abandoning myself to despair and homesickness [for Europe]," she wrote, "for I really feel as if it was intended I should be a Spaniard and quite a mistake that I was born in America." In another, she said, "I am in such low spirits over my prospects that although I would prefer Spain I should jump at anything in preference to America, and would look upon any of the places you mention as paradise."[5]

Her chance to return to Europe came late in 1871 when she received a commission from the Bishop of Pittsburgh (Pennsylvania) to copy two works in Parma for Pittsburgh's cathedral. (The present location of her copies is unknown.) She left for Europe with Emily Sartain, and stayed in Parma for eight months, studying with master printmaker Carlo Raimondi and immersing herself in the plentiful Correggios. Both aspects of her stay in Parma had an enduring influence on her later work. By 1872 she finally reached Spain, on her own, where she pursued her studies by copying the paintings of such old Spanish masters as Zurbarán and Velázquez. She described the Spanish school of painting to Sartain as "the most wonderful painting that was ever seen."[6]

In 1873 Cassatt met her mother in Paris and, after traveling on the Continent both with her and separately, she finally settled permanently in Paris in 1875.

During these years Cassatt regularly submitted work to the Paris Salon. The influence of Spain is evident in her submissions from 1872, *On the Balcony During Carnival,* and 1873, *Young Girl and Toreador,* both good examples of her pre-Impressionist style. Although the Salon jury accepted all of her submissions between 1872 and 1874, she started to become impatient with the Salon's artistic conservatism (and, in fact, her 1875 entry was refused).

Cassatt's increasing rejection of academic art appears to have had an adverse effect on her friendship with Emily Sartain. Although Sartain traveled to Parma with Cassatt in 1872, after four months she proceeded to Paris on her own and she began studies with the genre painter, Edward Luminais. When Cassatt returned to Paris in 1875, the competitive tension that is hinted at in some of their correspondence from the previous year—Sartain, for example, described Cassatt's 1874 Salon piece, *The Portrait of Mme Cortier,* as a "washed-out affair"[7]—reached a more full-blown state, and their friendship ended amidst mutual reproach.

The next five years were pivotal for Cassatt: she made Paris her permanent home, became affiliated with the Impressionists, and came into her early artistic maturity. Cassatt chose Paris as her residence in order to "look after her own interests," a pragmatic decision based on economics rather than affection, as she had never particularly liked the city. It proved to be a wise move. Paris was the center of artistic modernism and, after 1877, when Edgar Degas recognized her as a kindred spirit, Cassatt was accepted as one of the Impressionist group. Degas's reaction to her 1874 Salon submission was quite the opposite of Sartain's—upon seeing it for the first time, he is alleged to have exclaimed, "At last, someone who thinks as I do." In 1877, he asked her to make no further submissions to the Salon, to participate instead in the Impressionists' fourth exhibit (which took place in 1879, a year later than originally planned). Cassatt described her reaction to his request: "I accepted with joy. At last I was able to work with an absolute independence without thinking about the opinion of a jury. Already I knew who were my true masters! I admired Manet, Courbet and Degas. I hated conventional art. I began to live..."[8]

Cassatt's contributions to that show, *Lydia in a Loge, Wearing a Pearl Necklace* (1879) and *Little Girl in a Blue Armchair* (Plate 1), are prime examples of her early Impressionist paintings, with their careful recording of gesture and dramatic use of space and light. Cassatt received favorable notices as a result of her participation and, in 1882, her work was picked up by Paul Durand-Ruel, the most important dealer of Impressionist paintings at that time. After 1879 her output had increased dramatically, possibly because she was now in touch with a group of like-minded artists. Certainly it must have been encouraging

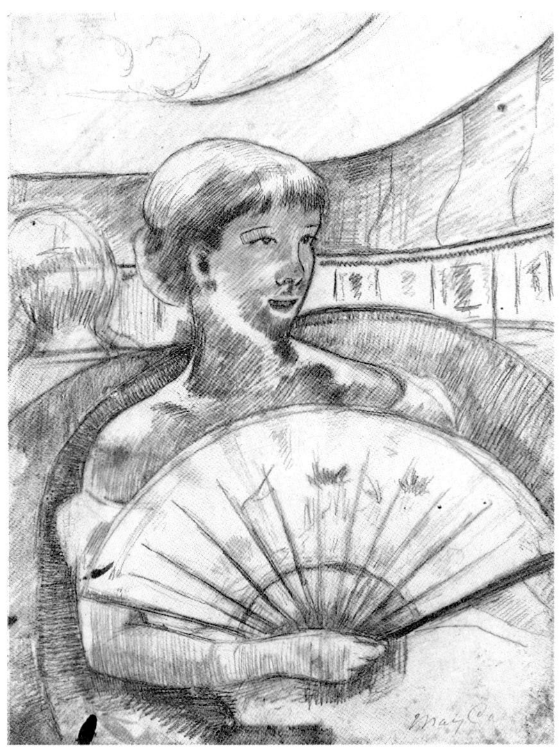

In the Opera Box (No. 3), 1880
Graphite
0.212 × 0.160 m (8 5/16 × 6⅜ in.)
Rosenwald Collection 1946.21.82.a

that her works had begun to sell. Some historians suggest that Cassatt's relationship with Degas was the cause of her increased productivity; the nature of their relationship has fascinated many and been the source of much speculation. Before her death, Cassatt burned Degas's letters and reputedly characterized the possibility of romantic involvement with "that common little man" as a "repulsive idea."

Cassatt's mother, father, and sister Lydia came to live with her in 1877, occasioning a significant change in her everyday life. Some critics have emphasized the deleterious effects of this arrangement, notably Frederick Sweet, who described it as an "eighteen-year bondage."[9] Cassatt certainly did become involved with the requirements of the failing health of all three of her relatives and their subsequent deaths, beginning with Lydia, who died of Bright's disease in 1882. Although she continued her professional career, it could be said that she assumed the typical role of the good, Victorian, unmarried daughter, a view corroborated in Cassatt's letters to her brother Alexander. In January 1884 she wrote from Tarragona on the Spanish Mediterranean coast, where she and her mother had gone to escape the Parisian cold, "My poor painting is sadly interrupted. I have no time now for anything

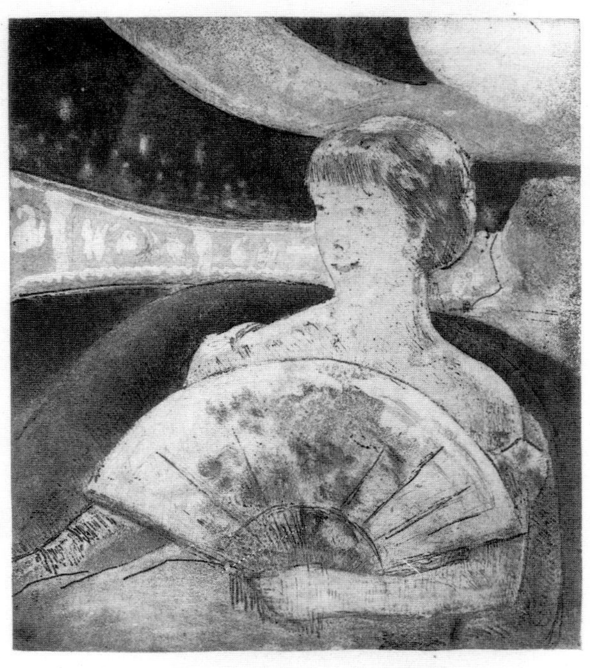

In the Opera Box (No. 3)
(Breeskin 22 iv/iv), c. 1880
Soft-ground etching, aquatint, and etching
0.197 × 0.177 m (7¾ × 7 in.)
Rosenwald Collection 1946.21.80

and the constant anxiety takes all heart out of me; my only hope is that this change will set Mother right for a time." Her letters also give ample evidence of tensions with her father; in the same letter she complains to Alexander that "[father] won't listen to a word I say," and two months later, she describes him as "harder to manage than he ever was in his life."[10]

It would be unfair, however, to consider Cassatt's living situation in purely negative terms. The fact that her productivity increased shortly after her family's arrival speaks for itself. The group formed a household which supported her emotionally and, as an unmarried woman dedicated to her art, gave her the opportunity to participate in family life without the pressure of a wife's responsibilities. Her parents enjoyed some relationships with her friends in the art world, sharing with Degas, for example, an active interest in horse-racing. Cassatt also remained in close contact with her brothers and their children, using various family members as artistic subjects, adding a personal aspect to her innovative treatment of domestic themes.

The subsequent years were marred by the deaths of both her parents, her father in 1891 and her mother in 1895, but they also saw the consolidation of Cassatt's artistic success and the spread of her reputation. She exhibited in three of the last four Impressionist exhibitions (1880, 1881, 1886), absenting herself (as did Degas) from the seventh, in 1882. Durand-Ruel gave Cassatt one-artist exhibitions in 1891 and 1893; in 1895 his gallery arranged her first individual exhibition in New York. She was commissioned to paint a large mural representing "modern woman" for the Court of Honor at the Women's Building (designed by the young architect Sophia Hayden) at the 1893 World's Columbian Exhibition in Chicago. (Mary Frances MacMonnies painted its companion, installed at the opposite end of the hall, showing "primitive woman.") Cassatt worked on this piece in a specially modified studio at the Chateau de Bachivillers during the summer of 1892, and described its feminist theme in a letter to Bertha Potter Palmer, the organizer of the Women's Building, as depicting "young women plucking the fruits of Knowledge and Science."[11] Although this mural unfortunately was lost at the end of the exhibition, Cassatt repeated aspects of its theme and structure in several works from the first years of the 1890s, most notably in her paintings of *Young Women Picking Fruit* (1891), and *Baby Reaching for an Apple* (1893), as well as in her print *Gathering Fruit* (c. 1893, Plate 22). These works from the last decade of the nineteenth century reveal a shift in Cassatt's style. Although she never treated form as loosely as some of her Impressionist contemporaries, Cassatt's later works took on more solid and monumental form than earlier ones, and were perhaps more dependent on Italian Renaissance frescoes as their source.

The most significant new influence on Cassatt's artistic development during this period, came from her exposure to Japanese prints. In 1890 Cassatt attended —several times—a major exhibition of Japanese *ukiyo-e* woodcuts at the École des Beaux-Arts; her visits with both Degas and Berthe Morisot have been well-documented. These "pictures of the floating world" of the Yoshiwara (pleasure district) in Edo (Tokyo) with their intimate glimpses into women's private domestic environments, were consistent with her own vision. She expressed her excitement about the prints to Morisot, to whom she wrote: "You could come and dine here with us and afterwards we could go to see the Japanese prints at the Beaux-Arts. Seriously, *you must not* miss that. You who want to make color prints you couldn't dream of anything more beautiful. I dream of it and don't think of anything else but color on copper."[12]

The influence of these works with their obvious love of pattern and plane can be seen in Cassatt's paintings from the 1890s, especially in *Modern Woman,* her World's Columbian Exposition mural, and the wonderful series of ten color etchings that she executed around 1891 (all of which are included in this volume Plates 10, 11, 13–20). She described her method for making these prints, of which she only printed eight to ten in a day, in two letters to the American collector Samuel P. Avery.

In one she explains that, "the set was done with the intention of attempting an imitation of Japanese methods. Of course I abandoned that somewhat after the first plate and tried more for atmosphere." In the other, she describes how she used Western printmaking techniques: "My method is very simple. I drew an outline in dry point and transferred this to two other plates, making in all, three plates, never more, for each proof—Then I put an aquatint wherever the color was to be printed; the color was painted on the plate as it was to appear in the proof."[13]

Many of Cassatt's contemporaries, including Degas, Henri Fantin-Latour, James Tissot, Morisot, Camille Pissarro, and Lucien Pissarro, were fascinated by the technical aspects of the Japanese woodcuts, and sought to emulate their lush colors and intricate patterns in their own works. Camille Pissarro was particularly impressed with Cassatt's results, which he described to his son Lucien as being "as beautiful as Japanese work, and it's done with printer's ink!"[14] Cassatt was able to approximate the visual effects of woodblock printing through western intaglio (etching) methods and to recast aspects of their composition and content into uniquely expressive works. On the basis of their technical virtuosity, the ten prints that belong to this series justify Cassatt's status as a master printmaker. They are in fact among the most distinguished of her work in any medium.

For the next twenty years Cassatt worked steadily. Although she was offered many prizes, she refused to accept any. As she wrote to Harrison Morris, the managing director of the Pennsylvania Academy of the Fine Arts, on learning that she had been named to receive an award, she remained loyal to the credo of the "old Independents" and their "principles . . . no juries, no medals, no awards."[15] In 1893, she had purchased the Chateau Beaufresne in Menil-Théribus (less than thirty miles from Paris), which remained her summer home for the rest of her life. Several girls from this region became her regular models (see, for example, *Sara Wearing a Bonnet and Coat,* Plate 26). After about 1910 she spent her winters in Nice in a rented villa.

Although she presented an awe-inspiring figure to biographer Achille Segard in 1912 when he interviewed her for his biography, her later years saw a decline in both her artistic productivity and general contentment. Her brother Alexander died in 1906; her other brother Gardner became ill during a trip to Egypt in 1910 and died in Paris in 1911. Cataracts began to curtail her productivity after 1912 and several operations were not successful; her later years were spent in near-blindness. Cassatt's loss of sight and resulting inability to work, along with the First World War, the deaths of her brothers and Degas (in 1917), and her own diabetes, left her reclusive and depressed in her later years. Her isolation and bitterness are sadly and clearly communicated in her letters from that period to Louisine Havemeyer. After an unsuccessful cataract operation in 1917, she despaired: "Oh Louie what a world we live in. I feel more and more that this is the end of civilization." Three years later she wrote: "One does get tired of the World and one wants to go when loneliness and struggle is all there is to look forward to. I have not done what I wanted to but I tried to make a good fight of it."[16]

Cassatt's distinctive treatment of the mother-child theme, and its place in her oeuvre, was recognized during her lifetime. Achille Segard, in fact, titled his 1913 biography, *Mary Cassatt: Un Peintre des Enfants et des Mères (Mary Cassatt: A Painter of Children and Mothers). Mother About to Wash Her Sleepy Child* (1880) is usually considered the earliest example of her use of this motif, and most of Cassatt's later works, after the turn of the century, focus on interactions between mothers and their children. Cassatt's frequent depiction of *maternités* has not always met with critical approval. Although today's critics no longer accept a sexist devaluation of the subject matter, some assert that Cassatt's depictions of late-nineteenth- and early-twentieth-century life do not present a significantly different, or less conservative viewpoint than the abundant late-eighteenth- and nineteenth-century images of "happy mothers," such as Jean Baptiste Greuze's *The Beloved Mother* or Jean Baptiste Chardin's *Saying Grace,* which extol the domestic virtue of the bourgeois family.

While it is certainly true that Cassatt selected her models from a limited range of ethnic background and class, her images of mothers and children distinguish themselves from those of both her predecessors and her contemporaries. In the western art historical tradition, the mother-child theme has been explored in innumerable idealized depictions of the Madonna and Child, in which nary a ruffle of discord is allowed. The concept of the pudgy bambino accompanied by his beatific mother developed during the Italian Renaissance in works by such artists as Luca della Robbia and Raphael. Cassatt's own early interest in Correggio surely must have influenced her continual return to this subject, although it must be stressed that Cassatt cast her images in secular, rather than religious terms, and depicted female as often as male children.

In her work, Cassatt used several approaches to avoid slipping into the generalized sentimentality that surrounds myths of maternity. Perhaps the most significant of these was her keen attention to specific detail. The anxious face of the mother in *The Boating Party* (Plate 23), the restless twist of the baby in *Mother About to Wash her Sleepy Child* (1880), the groggy gaze of the mother in *Breakfast in Bed* (1897), offer only a few examples of Cassatt's ability to break from stereotypical views. As an Impressionist, Cassatt was interested in capturing the fleeting gesture, rather than falling back on more conventional poses. In fact, she extended a willingness to transcribe the inelegant or unexpected in her depictions of children, allowing such works as *Little Girl in a Blue Armchair* (Plate 1) and *Children Playing on the Beach* (Plate 4) to avoid the pitfall of saccharine sweetness.

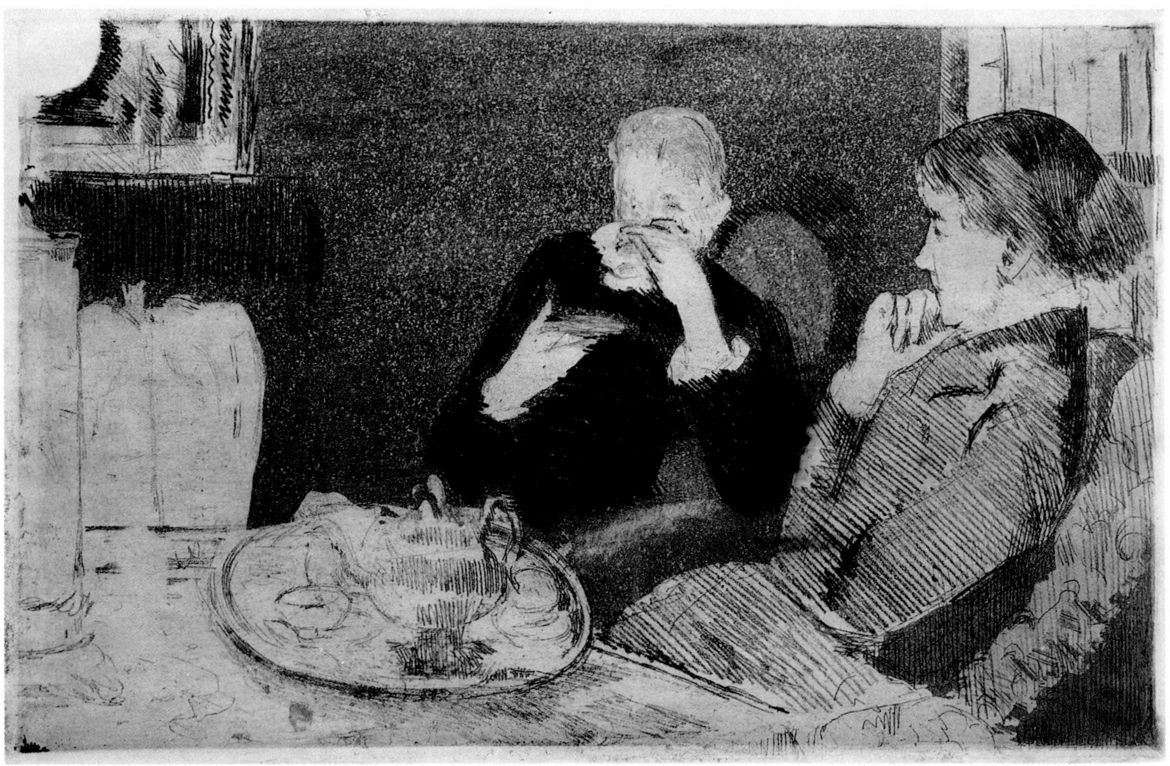

Lydia and Her Mother at Tea (Breeskin 69 v/v), 1882
Soft-ground etching and aquatint
0.177 × 0.280 m (7 × 11 in.)
Rosenwald Collection 1949.5.465

Cassatt's most effective pictorial device for expressing the closeness of the mother-child bond was to unite the figures into one solid form through continuous and contiguous contours. She used this construction in numerous paintings, such as *The Bath* (1892) and *Margot Embracing Her Mother* (1902) and in such prints as *Peasant Mother and Child* (Plate 24) and *Maternal Caress* (Plate 14). In these works and others, Cassatt often created continuous browlines for the figures to further emphasize their connectedness. She uses a similar approach in her one *paternité,* in which her brother Alexander and his son Robert are united into one, angular form (*Portrait of Alexander Cassatt and His Son Robert,* 1884/1885). Although these works are characterized by a universal monumentality, by skillfully manipulating the direction of the figures' gazes Cassatt is able to communicate particular aspects of the relationship between parent and child. In *The Bath,* for example, the mother and child both focus on the child's toes, supported by the mother's hand as she grasps the child's foot in order to wash it. In *Mother and Child* (Plate 27) both figures regard the child's reflection in the round mirror. On the other hand, Cassatt's figures often gaze in different directions, as in *Young Mother Sewing* (1902), in which the mother is absorbed in her sewing while a slightly disgruntled child leans her elbows on her mother's knees and gazes almost confrontationally at the viewer. In this and other works, Cassatt was not afraid to show the tension between intimacy and separation inherent to most relationships between mother and child.

Because Cassatt so frequently depicted *maternités,* it is inevitable to consider what that theme might have meant to her, especially since she remained childless. Some women artists — Harriet Hosmer, for example — referred to their works of art as their "children," but Cassatt is not known to have used that metaphor. Although it seems unlikely that her choice of subject expressed her frustration at not being a mother herself, she did state, late in her life, that "a woman's vocation in life is to bear children."[17] While Cassatt's expression of this sentiment needs to be taken with a healthy dose of skepticism, especially in light of her continual identification of herself as a professional artist, it bears an interesting relationship to strategies used by some nineteenth-century writers. Such writers as Elizabeth Stuart Phelps and Louisa May Alcott, who in their own lives remained single and childless, often created heroines who made more conventional choices. The tomboy and adventure-writer Jo March in Alcott's *Little Women,* for example, is married off to Professor Baer and consigned to telling stories to the boys in his school. Likewise, Cassatt — a professional artist of distinguished reputation — chose as her subject the domestic activities of child-rearing, acknowledging women's "proper" sphere.

Cassatt took as the subject of her art many other aspects of women's lives within the domestic sphere and in other socially acceptable milieus. In fact, Adelyn Breeskin has pointed out that when one considers Cassatt's complete oeuvre, there are "more portraits and figure studies of women than of mothers and children."[18] (The oarsman in *The Boating Party* (Plate 23) is a rare example of one of her very few images of adult men.) Sometimes Cassatt painted women alone and monumental, as in *Woman with a Red Zinnia* (Plate 12) or in *At the Opera* (1880), a visual discourse on seeing that represents a remarkable break with the usual depiction of women as the recipients of the male gaze. Many of Cassatt's other portrayals of women represent a similar departure, including portraits of her mother (see Plate 8), of Mrs. Riddle, and Miss Mary Ellison (see Plate 2). Other depictions of women show them engaged in a variety of personal activities, such as sewing, reading, or as in *The Letter* (Plate 13), sealing an envelope. In all these works, a central female figure is shown alone, self-absorbed, the subject of her own life: she is never the "other" in a male artist's story.

Cassatt was particularly perceptive in her exploration of the intimate relationships between women. In such works as *Young Women Picking Fruit* (1891), and *The*

Loge (Plate 3), Cassatt emphasized the women's close connection to each other through formal means—the "S" curve created by the figures in the former and the overlap of the two women in the latter. *The Loge,* in particular, employs the same compositional devices Cassatt uses to communicate the intimacy of the mother-child bond, including overlap, reflexive contours that form a single unit, and connected browlines. As in her depiction of mothers and children, Cassatt departs from conventional images through her close observation of specific details. Often she used women from her own family circle as her models, particularly her mother and her sister Lydia. Her mother, Katherine Kelso Cassatt became the subject of at least three very sympathetic paintings—*Reading "Le Figaro"* (c. 1878), *Mrs. Cassatt Reading to her Grandchildren* (1880), and *Portrait* (c. 1889). While she is shown as an active presence in the first two, despite the basically quiet nature of reading, the third (of which a related print is in this volume; see Plate 8) portrays the aging Mrs. Cassatt in a contemplative mood. Cassatt placed her sister Lydia in a number of situations—having tea with a friend, seated in an opera loge, working at a tapestry frame, crocheting in a garden. Interestingly, although most of these works were completed within only a few years of Lydia's death in 1882, usually Cassatt presented her beloved sister as the picture of health.

Griselda Pollock suggests that whether they are in a drawing room, a garden, or an opera house, the space that Cassatt's women inhabit becomes the locus of relationship.[19] In her essay "The Female World of Love and Ritual," Carroll Smith-Rosenberg describes how, in the eighteenth and nineteenth centuries "women lived in emotional proximity to one another," bound together by "intense bonds of love and intimacy." Their relationships characterized by "mutual dependency and deep affection," they provided a "supportive network" for each other that allowed them to "share sorrows, anxieties, and joys, confident that other women had experienced similar emotions."[20] That world was vividly chronicled in Louisa May Alcott's novel *Little Women,* so popular with its nineteenth-century audience and still a favorite of many twentieth-century adolescents. Cassatt, too, provided a convincing picture of women's close mutual ties within the domestic sphere, the private world in which she participated as a bourgeois woman in the late nineteenth century.

Both Cassatt and her contemporary Berthe Morisot, another woman artist who was closely associated with the Impressionist movement, used the Impressionist way of seeing to explore the domestic interior and the diverse relationships among its female inhabitants. Morisot, like Cassatt, showed women sewing, reading, chatting, picking fruit, and coiffing their hair. In their use of this milieu, called by Pollock "the spaces of femininity," they differed radically from their male colleagues, who were often attracted to the cafes and bars of the Parisian demimonde, inhabited by "fallen women," a world that was closed to Cassatt and Morisot, as to all proper "ladies."

Despite their similar iconography and Impressionist associations, Cassatt and Morisot's styles developed quite differently. Cassatt's relationship to the Impressionist movement was characterized by ambiguities stemming from the stylistic diversity among its various adherents. Cassatt considered herself an Independent (the name the group gave themselves) and thought that the term "Impressionist" was "a name which might apply to Monet, but can have no meaning when attached to Degas's name."[21] The term was first applied in the popular press with pejorative connotations, in response to a work titled, *Impression: Sunrise* by Monet in the group's first (1874) exhibition.

Whether called Impressionists or Independents, the work of the artists associated with the movement divides naturally into two different styles and approaches. Some artists, like Claude Monet and Camille Pissarro, were interested in capturing the immediate and evanescent effects of light. In general, these artists took the landscape as their theme and used "broken brush strokes" to denote the optical effects of the flicker of light. In their works, form is "dissolved" and the observer's eye becomes engaged in reconstructing the image. Degas, on the other hand, worked to communicate the fleeting gesture. Taking the figure in motion as his primary subject, he was greatly influenced by photography's ability to reveal the actual rather than the idealized gesture, particularly through cropping that implies not only the motion of the observed, but also that of the viewer. Furthermore, Degas was an excellent draftsman, rooted in the realist tradition, and committed to preserving the solidity of forms. In her focus on people and their interactions and her preservation of formal integrity, Cassatt stylistically and philosophically aligned with Degas rather than Monet.

For all their differences, however, the two Impressionist approaches are similar in that they exhibit a realistic perspective toward subject matter. All of the group of Independents attempted to portray the actual, contemporary world unadorned by such "higher" constructs as mythology, history, and religion. They strove to communicate the immediate perception, whether of changing light or fleeting gesture, rather than a generalized Ideal. In these ways, both subgroups radically challenged the academic conception of art and its making. Although now, over a century later, Impressionism has been universally accepted, in the nineteenth century it was considered a threat to the very nature of art.

Cassatt welcomed the revolutionary, political aspects of her affiliation with the Independents, relishing their challenge to conventional, academic art, and supporting their attempt to bypass the restrictions and repressions of the exhibition jury system. In addition to continually refusing

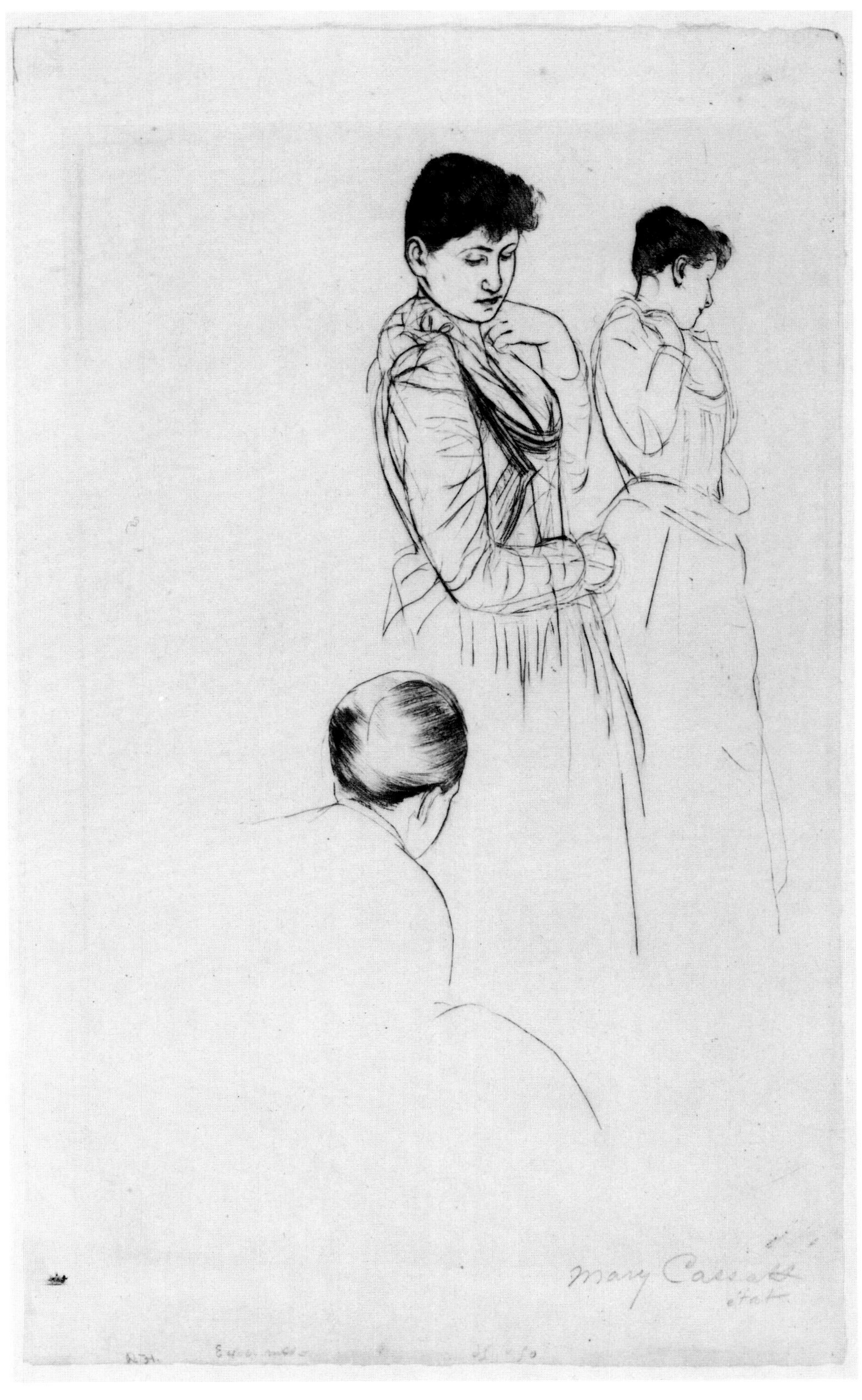

The Fitting (Mathews and Shapiro 1989, 9 i/vii), 1890/1891
Drypoint in black on medium-weight laid paper
0.435 × 0.267 m (17⅛ × 10½ in.)
Rosenwald Collection 1946.21.79

to accept awards, she would not participate on any juries. In 1905 she explained that she had never served on a jury because "I could never reconcile it to my conscience to be the means of shutting the door in the face of a fellow painter." She felt that the jury system encouraged mediocrity, whereas "it is essential to foster. . .the certainty that the one spark of original genius shall not be extinguished."[22]

While it is true that she lived her entire professional life in France and made her mark in the arena of Parisian modernism, it is also interesting to contemplate the extent to which Cassatt can be considered an American artist. Cassatt maintained ties with the American art scene throughout her career; she sent work back to the United States, and she was in regular contact with various American artists, museum and gallery directors, and other art-world figures. She made numerous recommendations to American dealers, institutions, and private collectors concerning the purchase of contemporary European art. Furthermore, to the extent that it is possible to isolate the characteristics of an American style, Cassatt's unique vision is not inconsistent with the concerns of her American contemporaries. With her interest in realism and her preservation of form through drawing, she can be compared to Thomas Eakins, her exact contemporary and also from Philadelphia, and to Winslow Homer, born less than a decade earlier.

Cassatt's letters paint a broad picture of her art and life, particularly in her correspondences with Emily Sartain during Cassatt's apprenticeship years and with Louisine Elder Havemeyer over the last forty years of Cassatt's life. Both these relationships ended abruptly because of ill feelings precipitated by misunderstandings in which Cassatt felt her professional integrity had been compromised. Cassatt's friendship with Sartain flourished while Cassatt was in the United States during the early 1870s. By 1875 they were no longer on speaking terms, their friendship unable to withstand their opposite stances on artistic modernism.

Cassatt met Louisine Elder (later Mrs. H. O. Havemeyer) through Sartain. Although "Louie" was ten years Cassatt's junior, they became fast friends. Havemeyer later served as chairwoman of the National Women's Party and encouraged Cassatt's participation in feminist activities, enlisting her to contribute works to the 1915 Suffrage Loan Exhibition at the Knoedler Gallery in New York, a show organized by Havemeyer in 1915 and discussed in their correspondence. Cassatt, for her part, guided the Havemeyers' art collecting, suggesting that Louisine, while still a teenager, use spending money to purchase her first Degas. She accompanied the Havemeyers on several trips to acquire Old Master paintings and on her recommendation, they purchased Manet's *Boating* (1874), now in the Metropolitan Museum of Art. In 1923 a misunderstanding about a series of drypoints, believed by everybody but Cassatt to be restrikes, made Cassatt bitterly eschew their friendship,

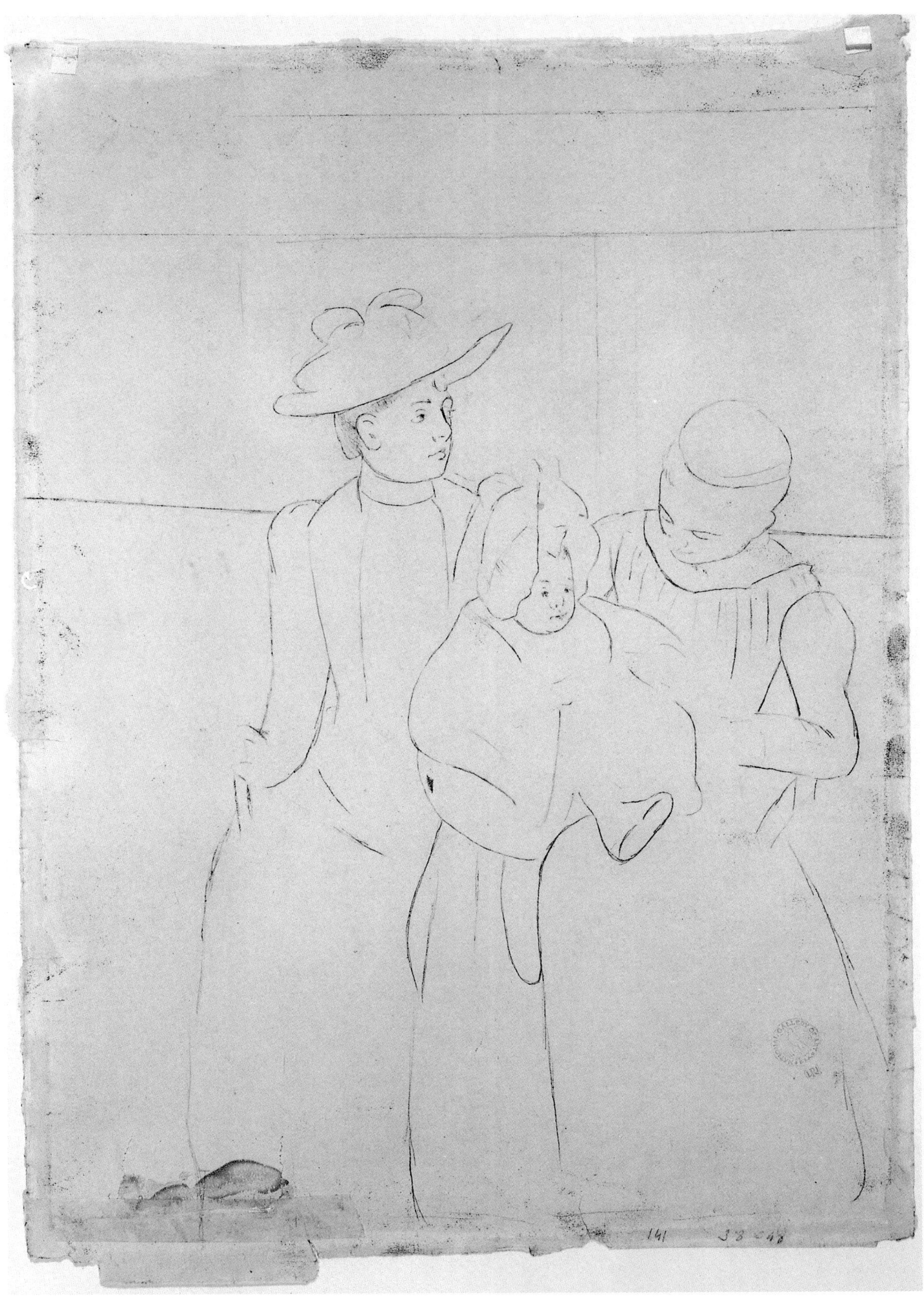

In the Omnibus, c. 1891
Transferred soft-ground medium on wove paper
0.379 × 0.271 m (14⅞ × 10¾ in.)
Rosenwald Collection 1948.11.51.b

although Louisine Havemeyer remained loyal to the end. Additionally, the frequent letters between Cassatt and the members of her family provide an invaluable source of information about the texture of her daily life and its economic aspects, as does her correspondence with other friends and professional associates.

As an artist, Cassatt was the consummate professional. Even while still a student, in a letter to her sister-in-law Lois (Alexander's wife), she distinguished between her sketching companion who was "only an amateur," and herself, one of the "professionals."[23] Pursuing art not for its external rewards, Cassatt affiliated herself with the artistic avant-garde of her time and produced works of innovative content. She also exerted a great influence on American collectors, persuading them to invest in the "new" art of the day, thus holding partial responsibility for bringing this work to the American public's attention. While Cassatt does not represent the only dedicated woman artist of her day, her renown is entirely justified.

NOTES

1 John Rewald, *The History of Impressionism* 4th rev. ed. (New York: The Museum of Modern Art, 1973); pp. 408–09 contain his longest sustained discussion of Cassatt.

2 Letter from Alexander Cassatt to his father, Robert S. Cassatt, 17 November 1869, quoted in Frederick Sweet, *Miss Mary Cassatt, Impressionist from Pennsylvania* (Norman, Okla.: University of Oklahoma Press, 1966), p. 14.

3 Quoted in Sweet, *Miss Mary Cassatt,* p. 150: "Mary Cassatt, sister of Mr. Cassatt president of the Pennsylvania Railroad, returned from Europe yesterday. She has been studying painting in France and owns the smallest Pekingese dog in the world."

4 Letter from Sara Hallowell to Bertha Potter Palmer, 6 February 1894, quoted in Nancy Mowll Mathews, *Cassatt and Her Circle, Selected Letters* (New York: Abbeville Press, 1984), p. 254.

5 Letters from Mary Cassatt to Emily Sartain, 22 May 1871 and 7 June 1871, quoted in Mathews, *Selected Letters,* pp. 70, 74.

6 Letter from Mary Cassatt to Emily Sartain, Madrid, 13 October 1872, quoted in Mathews, *Selected Letters,* p. 107.

7 Letter from Emily Sartain to John Sartain, Paris, 17 June 1874, quoted in Mathews, *Selected Letters,* p. 126.

8 Achille Segard, *Mary Cassatt: Un Peintre des enfants et des mères* (Paris: Librairie Paul Ollendorff, 1913), p. 8. Degas's response to Cassatt is quoted in Adelyn Dohme Breeskin, *Mary Cassatt: A Catalogue Raisonné of the Graphic Work* (Washington, D.C.: Smithsonian Institution Press, 1979), p. 18.

9 Sweet, *Miss Mary Cassatt,* p. 33.

10 Letters from Mary Cassatt to Alexander Cassatt, 5 January 1884 and 14 March 1884, quoted in Mathews, *Selected Letters,* pp. 177, 180.

11 Letter from Mary Cassatt to Bertha Potter Palmer, 11 October 1892, quoted in Mathews, *Selected Letters,* pp. 237–38.

12 Letter from Mary Cassatt to Berthe Morisot, April 1890, quoted in Mathews, *Selected Letters,* p. 214.

13 The first letter from Mary Cassatt to Samuel P. Avery is quoted in Breeskin, *Graphic Work,* p. 22. The second dated 9 June 1891, is quoted in Mathews, *Selected Letters,* p. 221.

14 Letter from Camille Pissarro to Lucien Pissarro, 3 April 1891, quoted in Mathews, *Selected Letters,* p. 219.

15 Letter from Mary Cassatt to Harrison Morris, 15 May 1904, quoted in Mathews, *Selected Letters,* p. 291.

16 Letters from Mary Cassatt to Louisine Havemeyer, 28 December 1917 and 22 May 1920, quoted in Mathews, *Selected Letters,* pp. 331, 333.

17 Quoted in Griselda Pollock, *Mary Cassatt* (New York: Harper and Row, 1980), p. 7.

18 Adelyn Dohme Breeskin, *Mary Cassatt: A Catalogue Raisonné of the Oils, Pastels, Watercolors, and Drawings* (Washington, D.C.: Smithsonian Institution Press, 1970), p. 15.

19 Griselda Pollock, *Vision and Difference: Femininity, Feminism and the Histories of Art* (London and New York: Routledge, 1988), p. 87. Pollock's chapter concerning women Impressionists is titled "Modernity and the Spaces of Femininity."

20 Carroll Smith-Rosenberg, "The Female World of Love and Ritual: Relations between Women in Nineteenth-Century America," in *Disorderly Conduct: Visions of Gender in Victorian America* (New York: Alfred A. Knopf, 1985), particularly p. 71.

21 Quoted in Pollock, *Mary Cassatt,* p. 21.

22 Letter from Mary Cassatt to John Beatty (then director of fine arts at the Carnegie Institute, Pittsburgh), 5 September 1905, quoted in Mathews, *Selected Letters,* p. 296.

23 Letter from Mary Cassatt to Lois Cassatt, 1 August 1869, quoted in Mathews, *Selected Letters,* p. 61.

1

Little Girl in a Blue Armchair

1878

Canvas
0.895 × 1.298 m (35¼ × 51⅛ in.)
Collection of Mr. and Mrs. Paul Mellon 1983.1.18

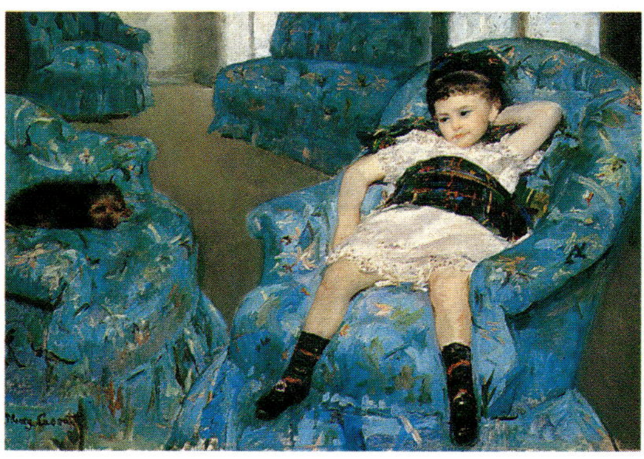

Cassatt showed this painting, one of her first in the Impressionist style, in the 1879 Impressionist exhibition, the first in which she participated. Its emphasis on texture, pattern, and gesture expresses concerns that Cassatt continued to explore in later works.

The room's receding space is constructed with great drama. The bold use of cropping, and the oblique angle from which the viewer enters the space, were devices also used by Edgar Degas to communicate the experience of the fleeting glance. In fact, Cassatt executed the painting during the year in which she met Degas and, in an oft-quoted letter (probably of 1903) to the art dealer Ambroise Vollard, Cassatt remarked that Degas had even worked on the background. In the same letter she recounts that she submitted it to the 1878 Grand Exposition in Paris, whose jury "of three people, one of whom was a pharmacist," rejected it. The following year Cassatt, with this painting, began to exhibit with the Independents, as the Impressionists called themselves.

One of Cassatt's earliest depictions of children, the little girl is obviously of central importance to the painting's structure and meaning. Cassatt sets up a dynamic polarity between the girl on the right-hand side of the picture surface and the dog—one of her beloved griffons—on the left. Each figure is situated in a foreground chair, and a visual analogy is created between the curve of the sleeping dog's body and the curve of the tartan that has ridden up at the girl's hips, both forms dark in contrast to the lighter blue of the chairs.

The girl's pose is decidedly inelegant. She is sprawled in the chair, her skirt in disarray, one arm akimbo, in what her mother must have repeatedly warned her was an unladylike position. Although in the hands of some artists erotic aspects of the image might have been exploited, Cassatt eschews that here. The bored, squirmy, confrontational demeanor of the child prevents any reading of her as a passive object. Instead, the viewer tends to identify with her expression of free-spirited rebelliousness, as Cassatt probably did herself.

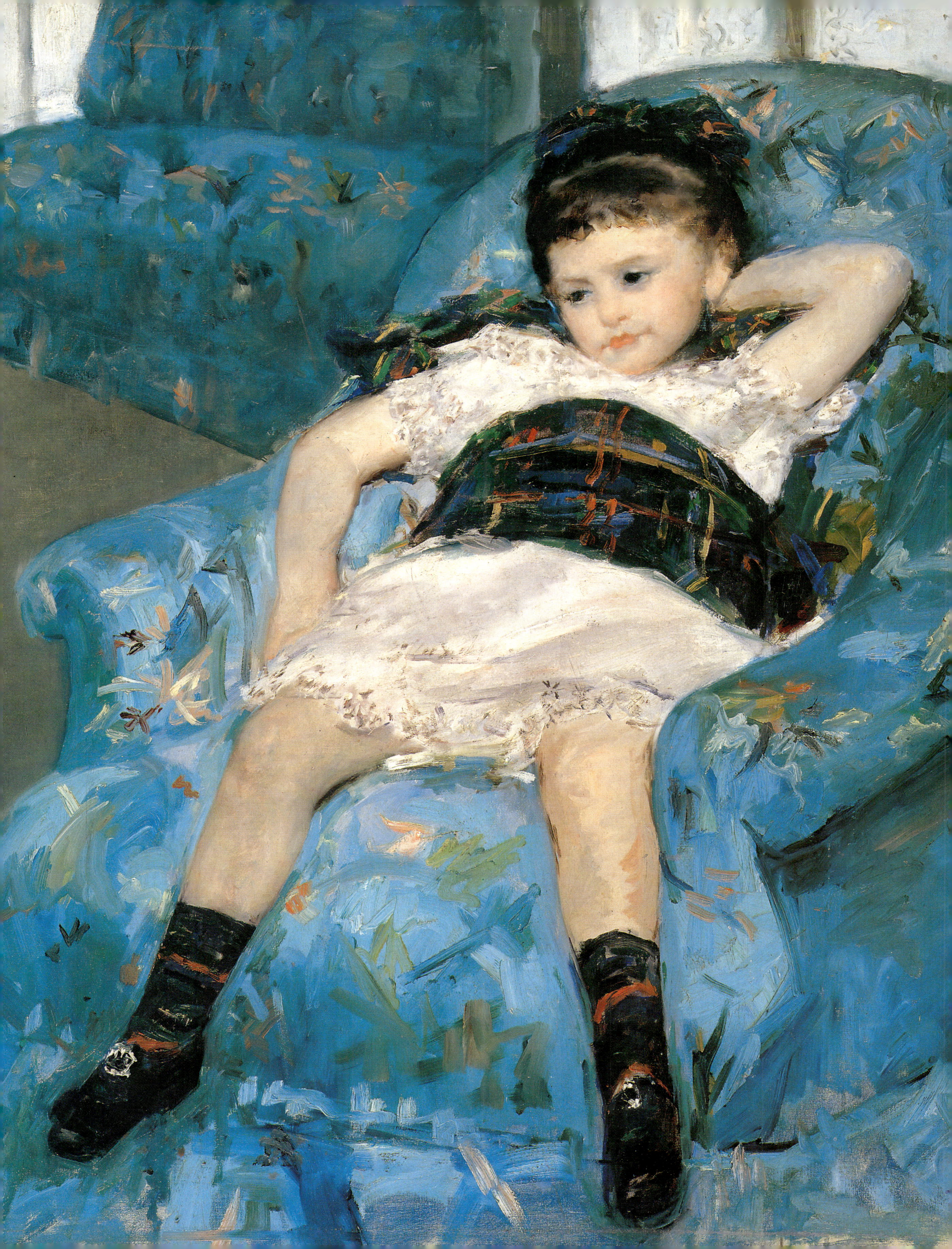

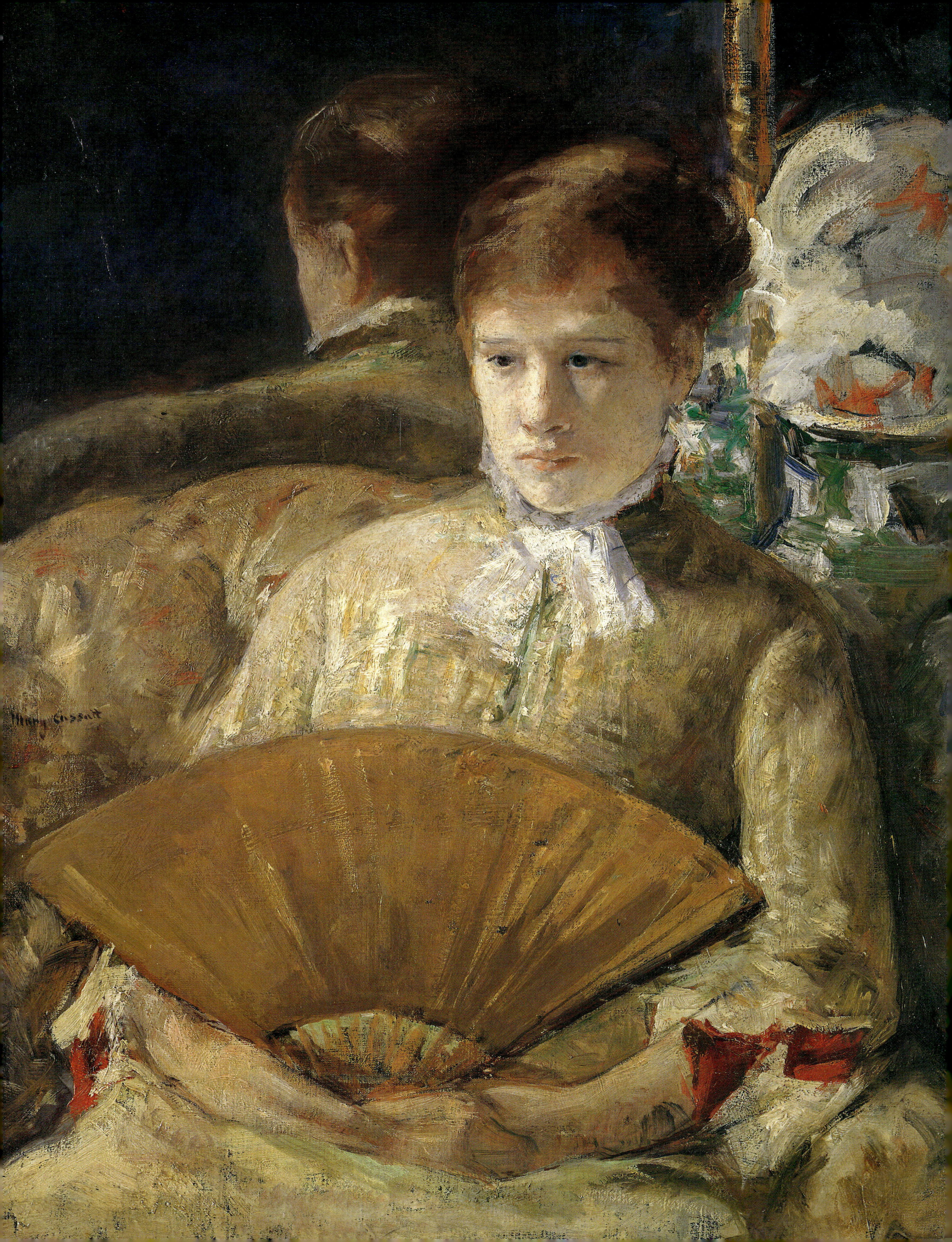
Mary Cassatt

2

Miss Mary Ellison

c. 1880

Canvas
0.850 × 0.653 m (33½ × 25¾ in.)
Chester Dale Collection 1963.10.95

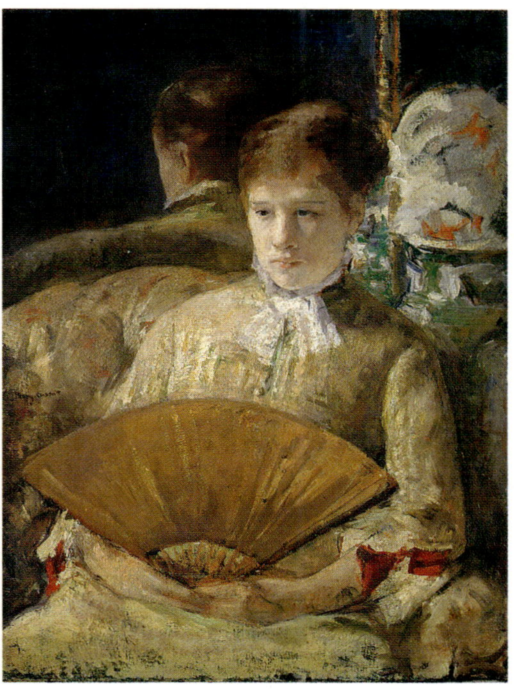

This is actually Cassatt's second portrait of Mary Ellison, who later became Mrs. William H. Walbaum. The two women met through Cassatt's lifelong friend and correspondent, Louisine Elder (later Mrs. H. O. Havemeyer), when as a young woman Ellison lived in the same Parisian *pension* as Louisine and her sisters. Cassatt's earlier painting (1877) showed Ellison working her embroidery. Ellison's daughter subsequently compared the two works, writing that "the portrait in Washington [the one reproduced here] is a dreamy young girl, the one I have is the vital, enthusiastic one which is to me much more my mother. . . ." (Breeskin, *Oils, Pastels, Watercolors, and Drawings,* p. 58).

In fact, the pensive mood of the sitter, lost in her own thoughts, is noteworthy. During the early 1880s, Cassatt painted many works with solitary women caught in various activities, including several images of her sister Lydia. In each case, the subjects are self-contained, possessing their own characteristic and independent inner lives. Along with the slightly later painting *Girl Arranging Her Hair* (1886, Plate 6), these works present sympathetic and diverse views of women and their private activities, thus departing from more stereotypical images of women as objects existing for the pleasure of the male gaze.

Technically, this work is a tour de force. The brushwork, particularly in the upper right corner, is especially lush and painterly. As in *The Loge* (1882, Plate 3), Cassatt uses the arc of the fan as a unifying compositional device, echoed in the curves of Miss Ellison's shoulders and the back of the settee. Cassatt also reveals here her fascination with mirrors and their reflections. Manet's 1881 painting, *The Bar at the Folies Bergères,* also quite a bravura piece, used a mirror in a similar way, but his setting placed women in the public demimonde rather than the private sitting room.

3

The Loge

1882

Canvas
0.799 × 0.639 m (31½ × 25⅛ in.)
Chester Dale Collection 1963.10.96

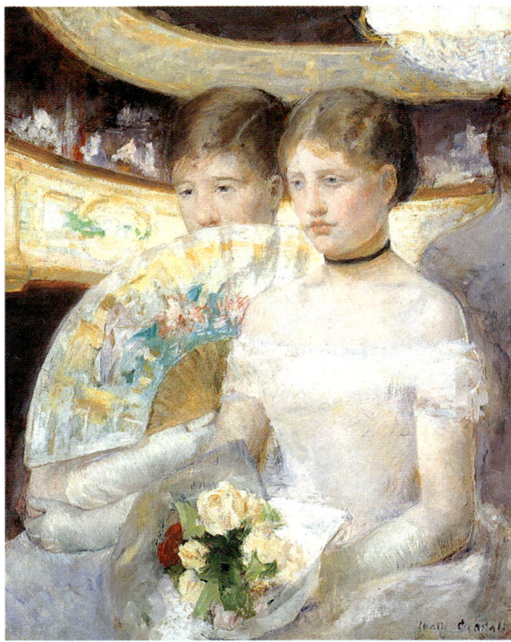

Cassatt used the opera house as a setting for works in several media, including this work and the paintings *At the Opera* (1880) and *Lydia in a Loge Wearing a Pearl Necklace* (1879). *The Loge* shows two women seated side by side with the loge reflected in a mirror behind them. A fashionable venue, the opera was one of the few public spaces that was acceptable for proper ladies. Cassatt produced four graphic works in developing the tightly structured composition of this painting.

This work explores one of Cassatt's favorite themes, the intimacy between women. Although these women do not look at each other, they form a single monumental shape—their heads lean together and their bodies overlap. The fan held by one figure contributes to this effect by reflecting the shape of the other's shoulder. The fan also works compositionally with the arcs of the balcony in creating a series of opposing curves that stabilize in the area of the heads, on which they focus the viewer's attention.

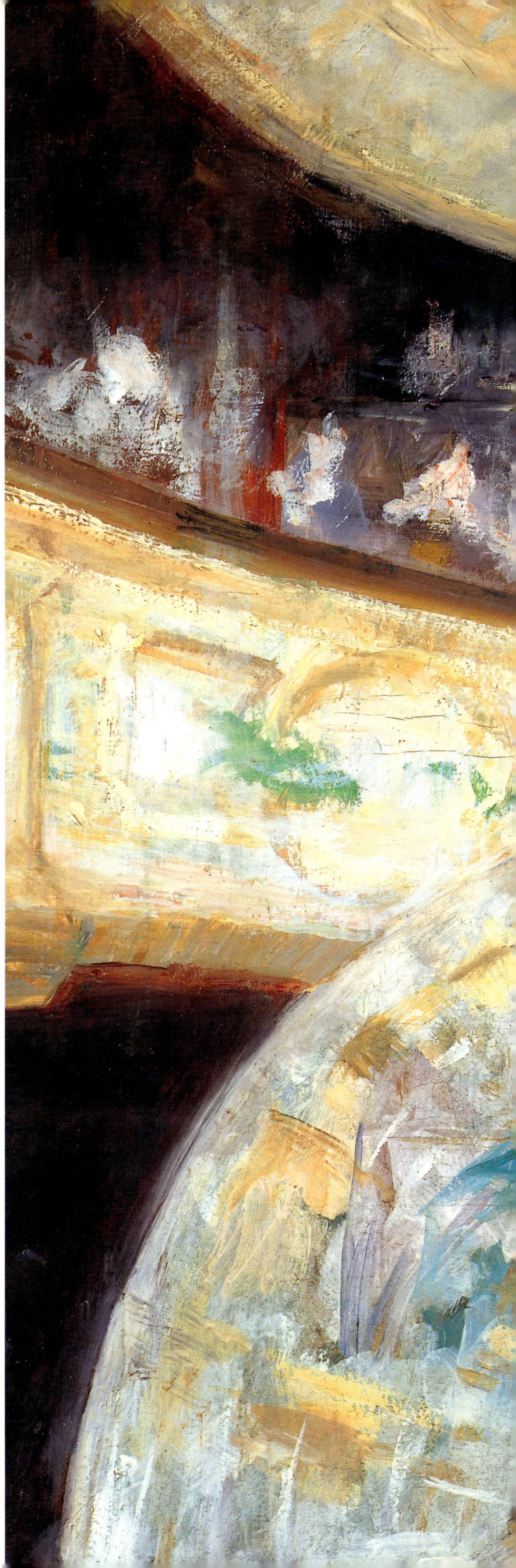

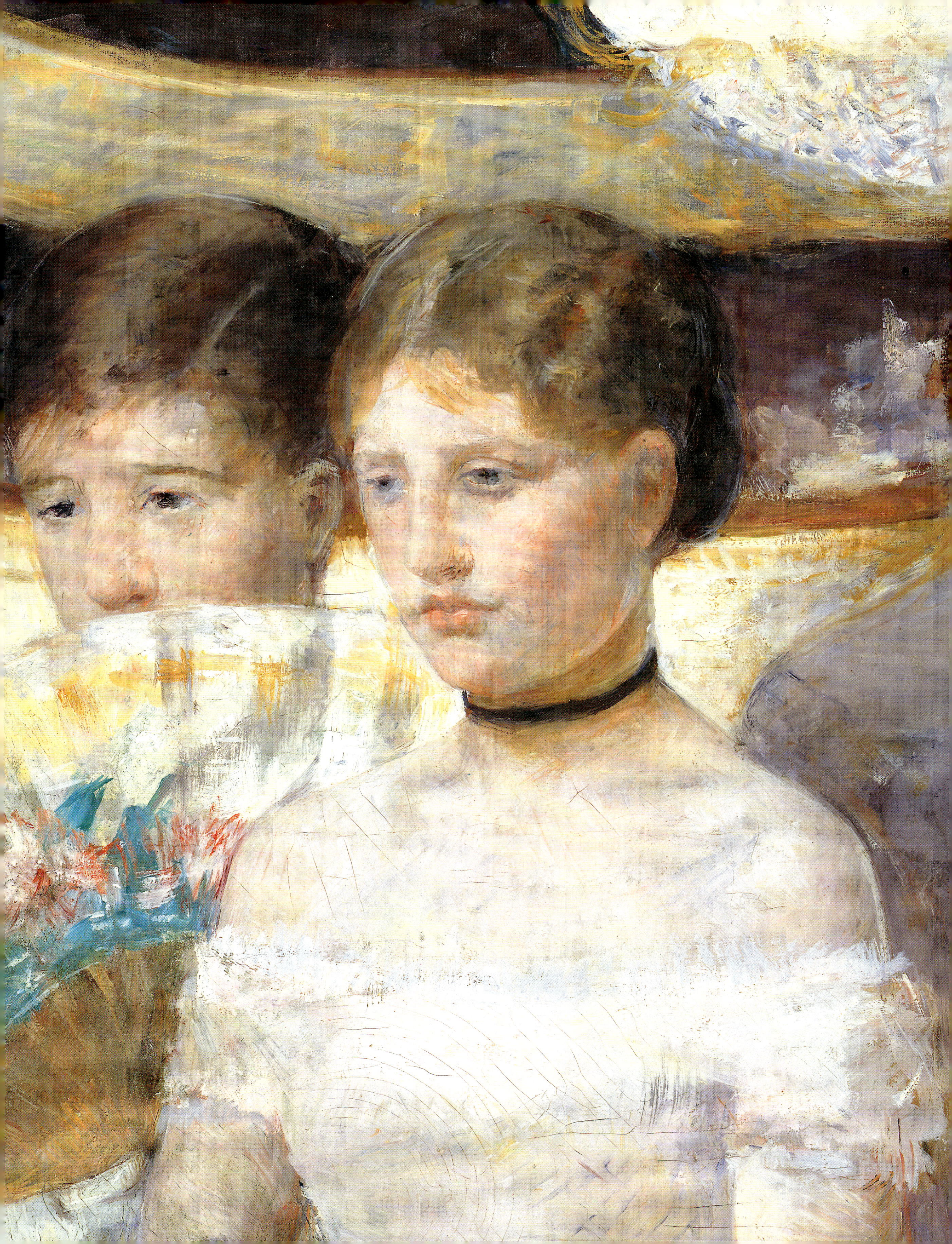

4

CHILDREN PLAYING ON THE BEACH

1884

Canvas
0.974 × 0.742 m (38⅜ × 29¼ in.)
Ailsa Mellon Bruce Collection 1970.17.19

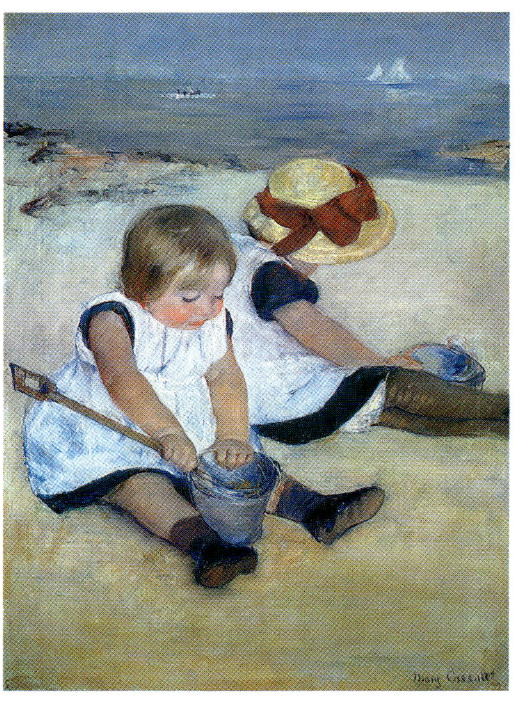

This work reveals Cassatt's characteristic use of the Impressionist idiom. Like Edgar Degas, Cassatt's claim to Impressionism rested on her ability to capture the fleeting gesture, glimpsed in passing. Each child's self-absorption helps to communicate that effect, as does the hat which hides one child's face—they are caught, unposed, in the midst of an activity. Impressionists such as Claude Monet, looking at this same scene, would have emphasized the effects of light on the sea. Although Cassatt is more interested in exploring the human action, this work does contain some passages with particularly loose handling of paint, as in the streaks of orange and dark brown on the left-hand border where the sea and shore meet.

The special magic of this work lies in the way that Cassatt brings the viewer down to the level of the two children as they sit at the beach, playing with their pails in the sand. They are prominent masses, large forms that dominate the picture surface; thus we see this scene from their point of view. The work's vertical orientation enhances this effect. While most landscapes—and particularly seascapes—are oriented horizontally to emphasize spatial expansiveness, in this work, Cassatt strives for the opposite impact. By showing only a small bit of the ocean and an even smaller area of sky, with a very high horizon, and by cropping the feet of one of the girls on the right-hand border, she creates the effect of an enclosed and boxed-in space, the area in which the children play.

Cassatt further endears these children to the viewer through her emphasis on rounded forms. Their pudgy cheeks, the awkward grasp of their hands on the pails, their little legs, clumsily outstretched, are irresistible. The particular activity, a child digging in the sand at the beach on a summer's day, is also charmed, epitomizing the essence of childhood, both our own and our children's.

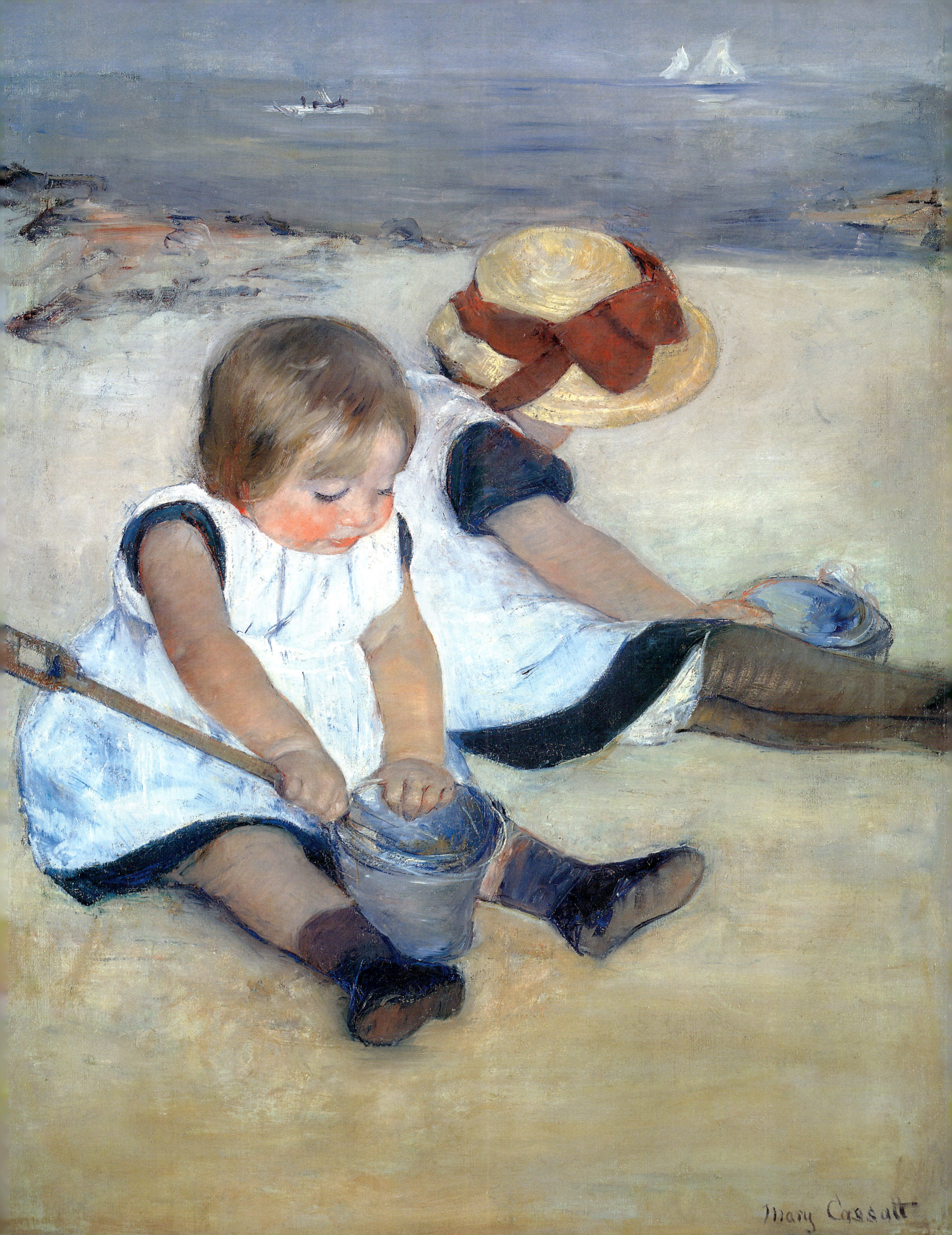
Mary Cassatt

5

Child in a Straw Hat

c. 1886

Canvas
0.653 × 0.495 m (25¾ × 19½ in.)
Collection of Mr. and Mrs. Paul Mellon 1983.1.17

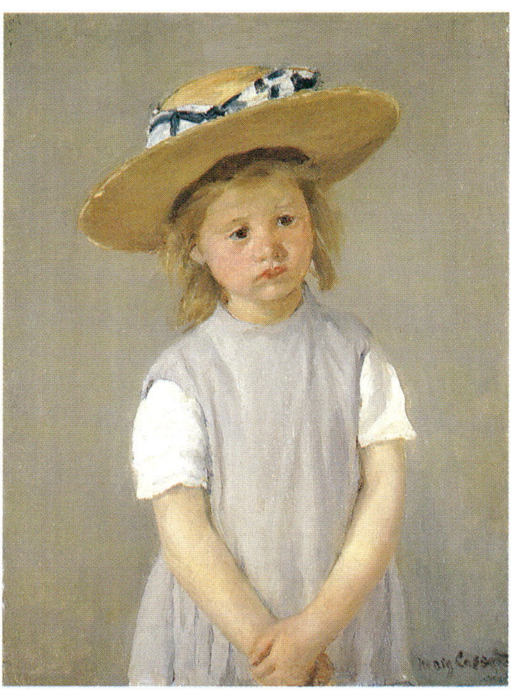

This is one of the earliest examples of a theme, well-represented in this volume, that Cassatt was to return to many times: an appealing young girl whose face is offset by an interesting hat. It is uncertain who the model for this figure might have been, although her simple outfit and straw hat have suggested to some that she is of rural origins, a local girl like several of Cassatt's other young models.

The predominance of neutral tones and lack of background articulation make this work unusual. Cassatt has built the painting with subtle variations of grays and ochers. The girl's gray pinafore, with its lavender cast, is barely contrasted with the background, another gray, but one with a suffusion of ocher that echoes the girl's hat and hair. The area of her cheeks and lips is emphasized by a light-handed use of pink, which helps to draw our attention to her facial expression.

This image of a small, young person against a grayish ground cannot help but remind the viewer of Édouard Manet's image of *The Fifer* of twenty-odd years earlier, although the figure in that work is considerably more flattened than Cassatt's. The little girl here appeals all the more due to the artist's emphasis on her rounded, pudgy forms: the curve of her head, of her shoulders, and of her folded arms, echoed, of course, by the shape of the hat.

Cassatt's genius at capturing the moods of childhood also shows here. With an absolutely bare economy of means, Cassatt convinces us to believe in this little girl with the pouty, questioning, and perhaps worried look on her face.

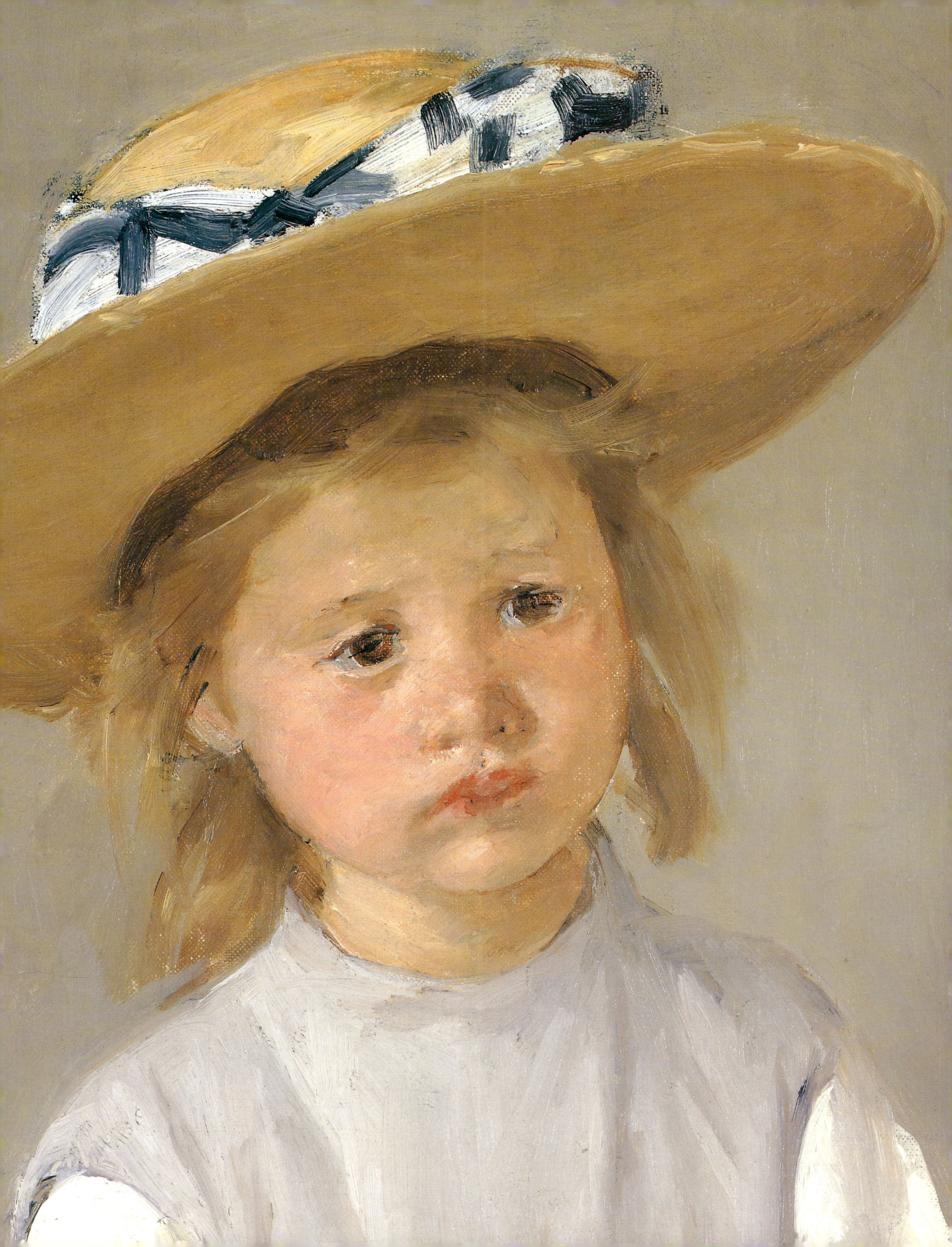

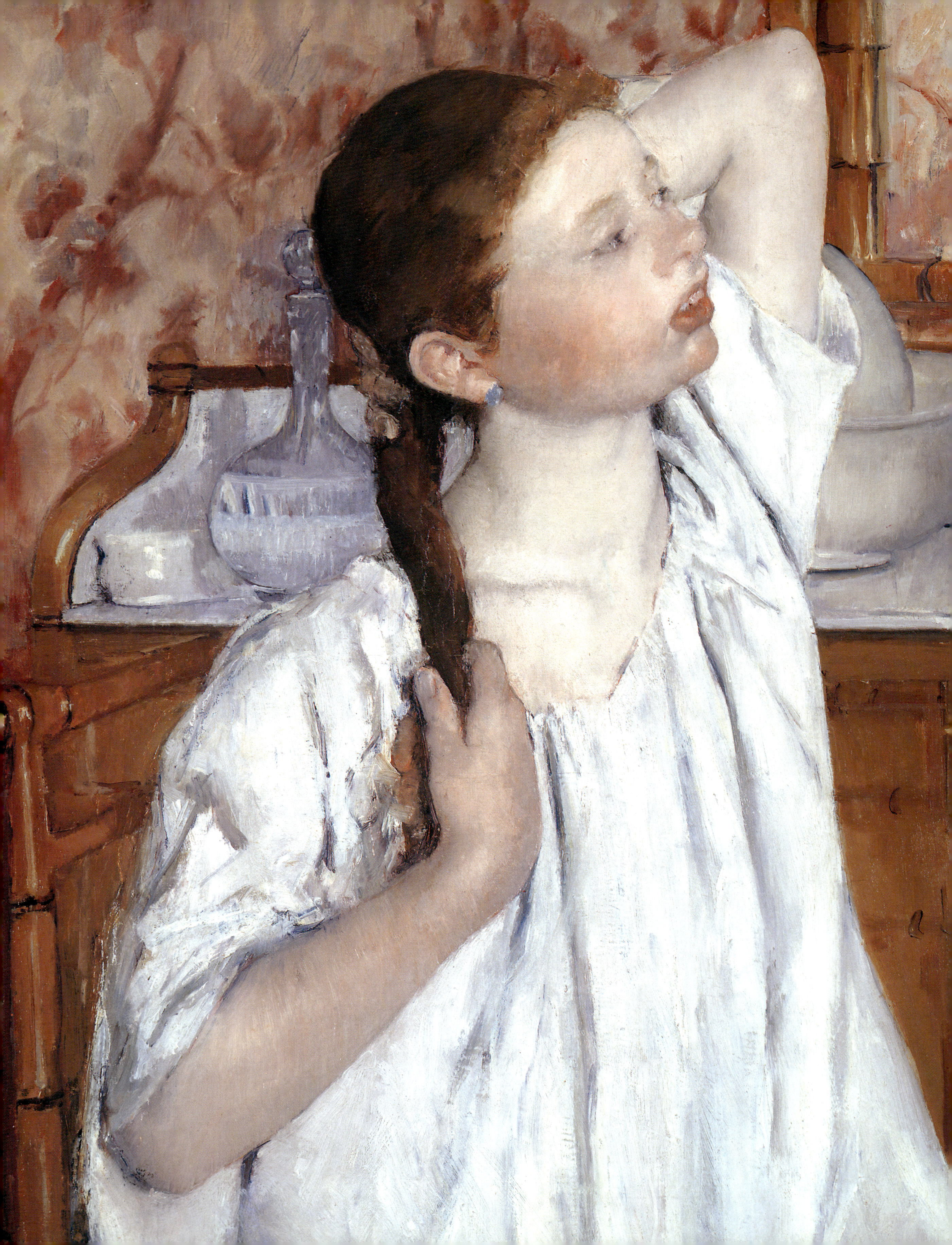

6

Girl Arranging Her Hair

1886

Canvas
0.750 × 0.623 m (29½ × 24½ in.)
Chester Dale Collection 1963.10.97

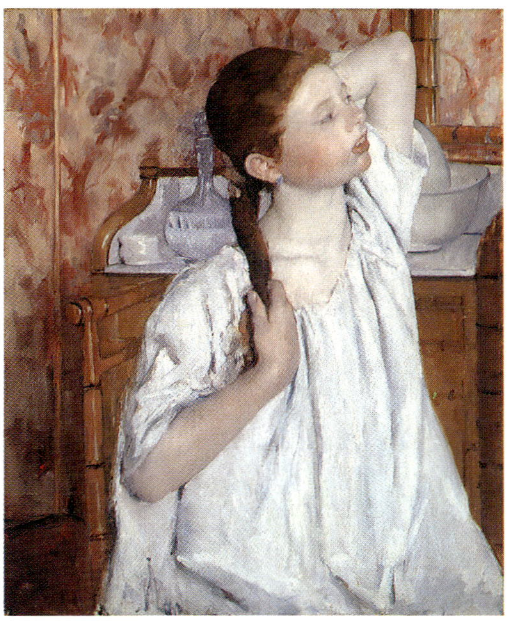

This work, shown in 1886 at the eighth and last Impressionist exhibition, was allegedly painted in response to an argument between Cassatt and Edgar Degas concerning his disbelief in women's ability to distinguish style in art. Cassatt decided to prove Degas wrong by painting a beautiful work about a subject considered unlovely, a young serving girl. In both composition and tone, the resulting work is certainly aesthetically appealing.

The theme of women engaged in their *toilette*—coiffing their hair, examining themselves in the mirror—was a favorite of both Cassatt and Berthe Morisot. Both artists took their inspiration from the subject matter of Japanese prints, later explored by Cassatt in a series of prints which is represented in this volume. Perhaps Cassatt and Morisot were especially responsive to the view of women's private lives presented in the Japanese works because of its similarity to conventions with which they were familiar in their own lives and those of their female associates. The Japanese influence in this work extends beyond its subject to the use of pattern in the wallpaper and the resultant flattening of space.

The painting offers a significant alternative to the stereotypical presentation of the female figure as a beautiful object of contemplation. Cassatt has not attempted to prettify the girl or to make her inviting to the viewer's gaze. Rather, the young servant's idiosyncratic features—her odd mouth, large teeth, and wide nose—are clearly delineated, and her arms are caught in an awkward position. Most notable, Cassatt presents the girl in a private setting, not exposed for the benefit of the viewer; her action is self-contained, not provocative. As she gazes to the left, presumably at her reflection in an unseen mirror, she appears to be lost in a private reverie. Here as in other works, we can see how the characteristic Impressionist interest in faithfully recording the specific gestures of everyday life allowed Cassatt to break with pictorial conventions.

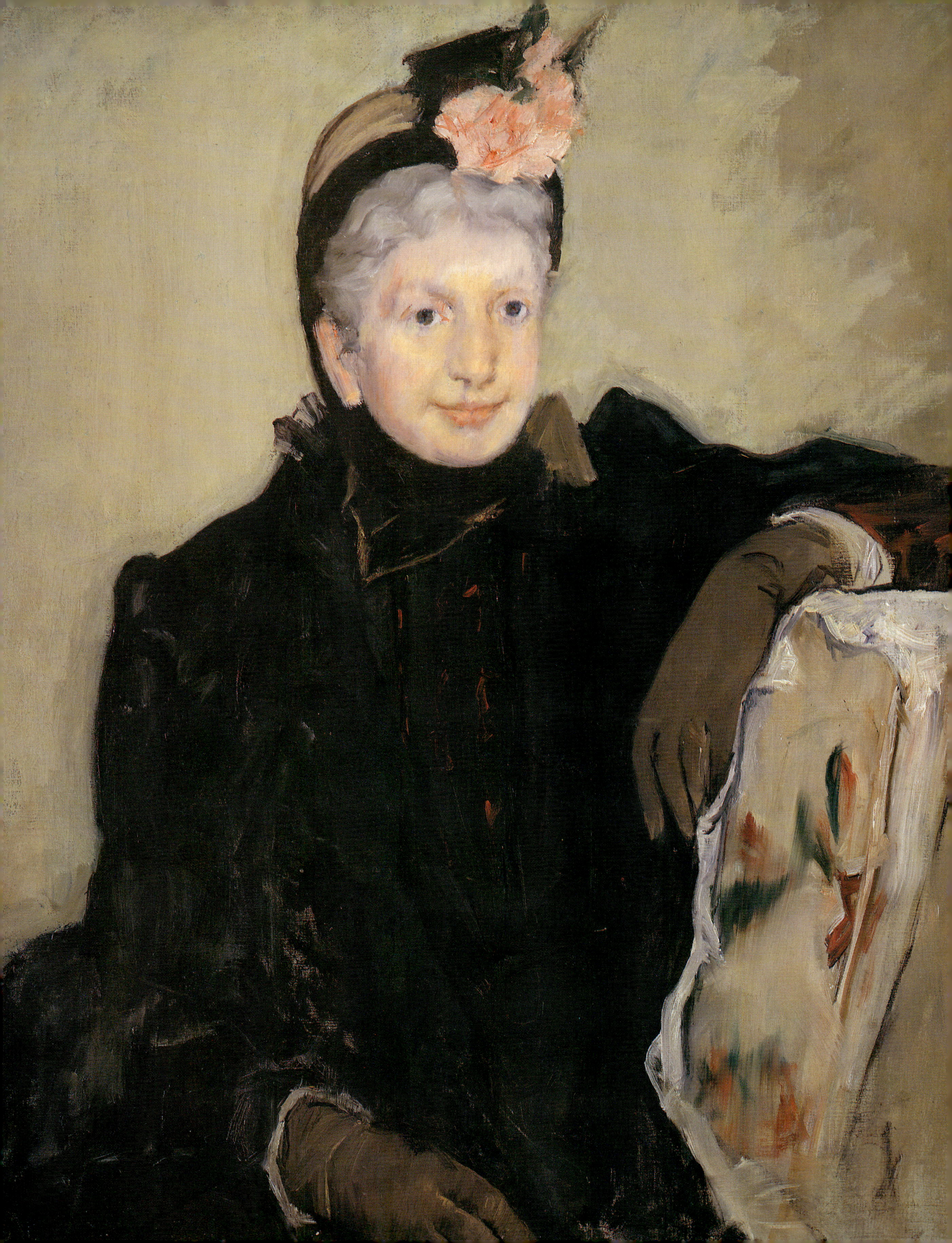

7

Portrait of an Elderly Lady

c. 1887

Canvas
0.728 × 0.603 m (28⅝ × 23¾ in.)
Chester Dale Collection 1963.10.7

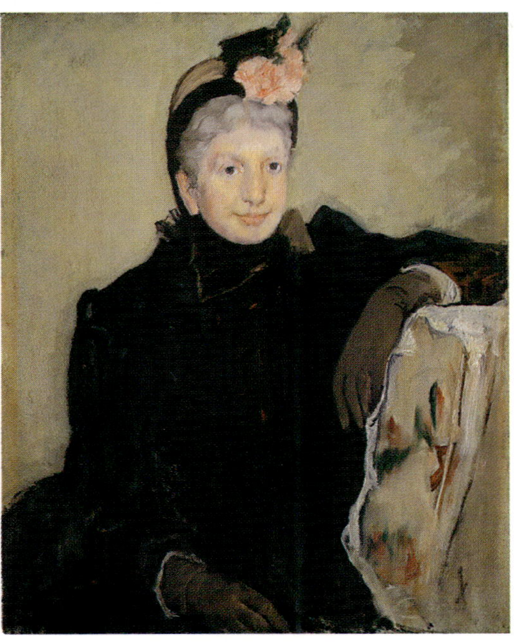

Cassatt gave this animated portrait of an elderly lady seated on an upholstered chair to her trusted domestic servant and companion of many years, Mathilde Vallet. It was purchased in 1927 by the American collector Chester Dale at the Parisian sale of Vallet's collection, consisting of works that were either given to her by Cassatt or, in some cases, rescued by her from oblivion.

Its subject shows Cassatt's ability to render with sensitivity women of varying ages. It represents a departure from the western artistic tradition which treats harshly the effects of the aging process on women, with older women usually stereotyped as crones. This work resembles Cassatt's portrait of Mrs. Robert Moore Riddle, her mother's cousin, *Lady at the Tea Table,* completed two years earlier; although Cassatt portrays Mrs. Riddle with a somewhat stern demeanor, she gives the woman in this work a pleasant, agreeable smile. The painting is consistent with other of Cassatt's works from this period whose subjects are solitary women in possession of their identities, and it bears a marked resemblance to an earlier portrait, *Young Woman in Black* (1883), whose subject seems to be seated on the same chair.

Although the figure's pose is fully frontal and hence more static than many of Cassatt's images, the work's drama is created through formal means, seen particularly in the contrast between the dark tones of the figure's dress and the highlight of the vivid pink rose in her bonnet. This portrait was originally referred to as a study, perhaps due to Cassatt's use of quick, notational strokes—especially to denote the floral pattern of the couch—which also contribute to the sense of vitality that emanates from this woman of advanced years.

8

Portrait of the Artist's Mother

(Mathews and Shapiro 1989 4 iv/iv)
c. 1889

Soft-ground etching and aquatint in
light brown, yellow, and green
0.352 × 0.210 m (13⅞ × 8½ in.)
Rosenwald Collection 1946.21.90

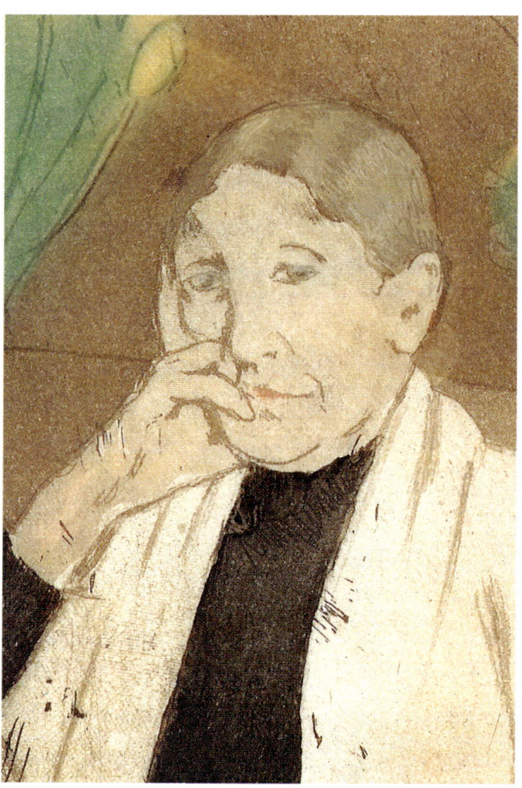

This portrait of Cassatt's mother, Katherine Kelso (Mrs. Robert S.) Cassatt, is executed in dark tones, its subtle color added only in the final two states. The only print included in this volume that predates Cassatt's visit to the Japanese woodcut exhibition, it reveals by comparison the dramatic effect of the Japanese work on her own.

This portrait is closely related to a painting of Mrs. Cassatt from the same year, of which this is a reverse image. Both works feature the figure in the same pose and setting, seated in front of a mirror with a vase of flowers to the side; in each she makes the same gesture, pensively resting her head on one hand. The print's impact differs slightly: the subject's expression is communicated more harshly—her eyebrow seems more arched and her lips more pursed—perhaps because of the greater linearity of the printing medium.

It is difficult to encounter such a somber, pensive image of an artist's mother without recalling James Abbott McNeill Whistler's famous work from 1872 of the same title. While he was interested in the subject as "an arrangement in black and gray," Cassatt was more concerned with exploring its psychological aspects, particularly as they relate to the idea of the ages of women. In this context, it is interesting to compare the print to two earlier portraits Cassatt made of her mother, the first when Mrs. Cassatt was more than a decade younger, in which she is presented as a far more active figure. In *Mrs. Cassatt Reading to Her Grandchildren* (1880), she is the center of her grandchildren's rapt attention, and *Reading "Le Figaro"* (c. 1878) shows her brow furrowed in concentration, her pince-nez perched on her nose, as she reacts to the news of the outside world. In this later work, however, Mrs. Cassatt has turned inward, as she holds her handkerchief in her lap and her head in her hand.

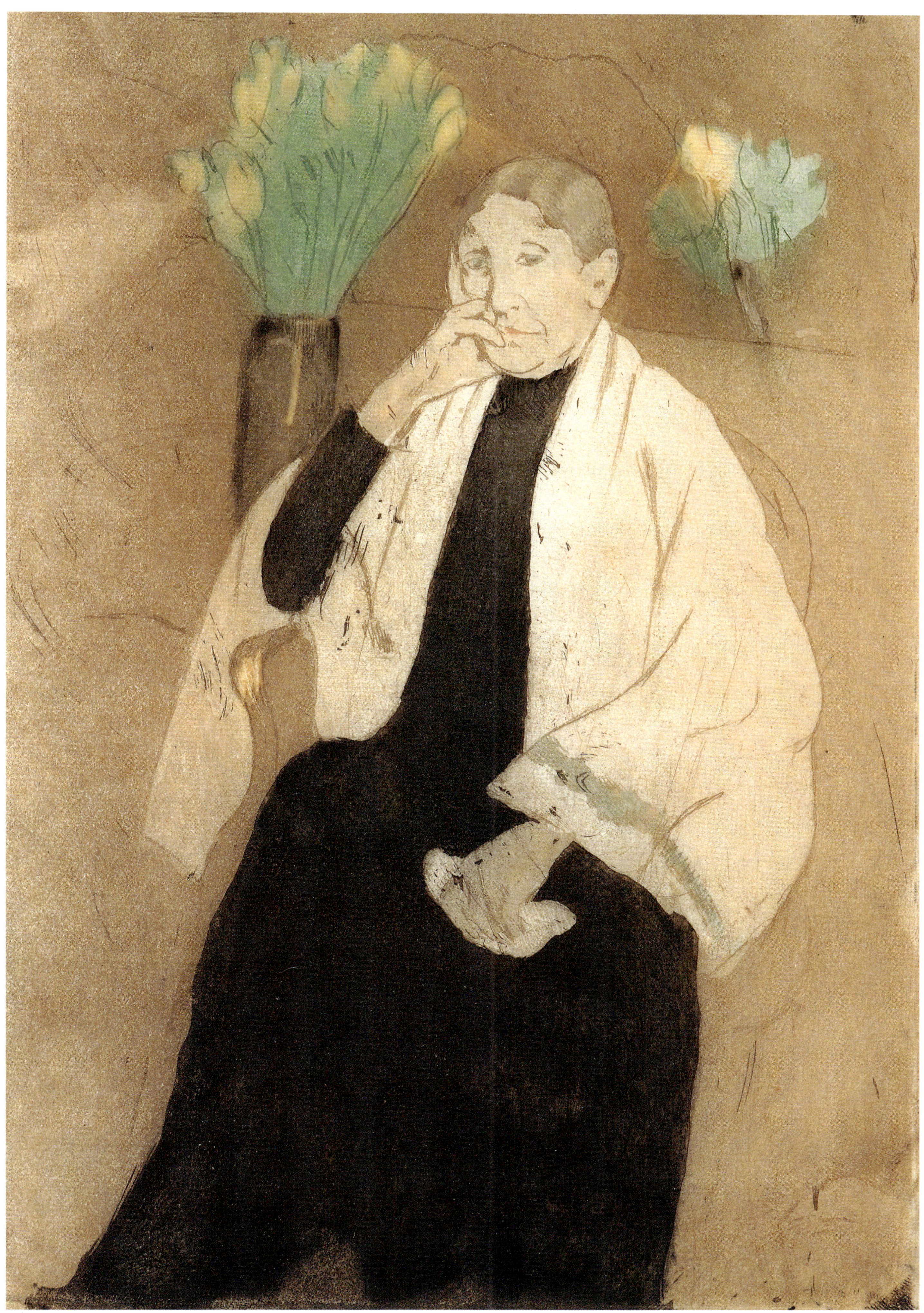

9

The Black Hat

c. 1890

Pastel
0.610 × 0.455 m (24 × 18 in.)
Collection of Mr. and Mrs. Paul Mellon 1985.64.81

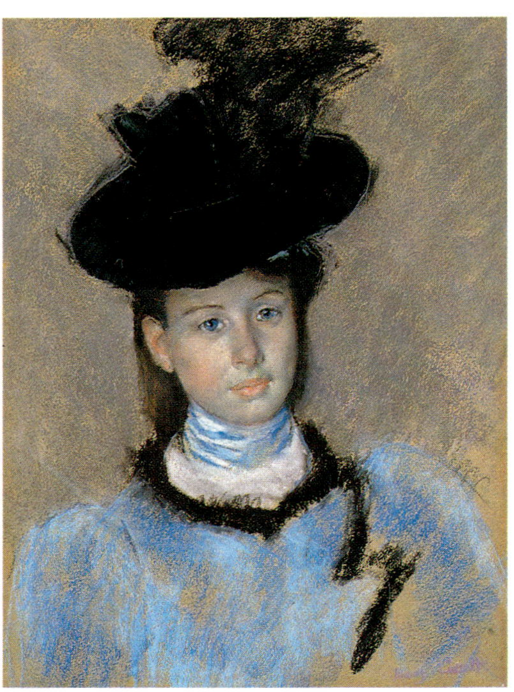

Also called *Portrait of a Young Girl in a Black, Plumed Hat,* this work is one of many by Cassatt that take as their subject a bust-length female figure crowned with an exotic headpiece. Although slightly later in her career Cassatt used preadolescent girls as her models, the model here is somewhat older, as in other works on the theme from the 1880s and 1890s. Some related images suggest a visit to the milliner's by showing the subject tying her bonnet or arranging her veil; this sitter, however, not engaged in any activity, confronts the viewer head-on.

The work is interesting in its use of the pastel medium. Because pastels are pure pigment they allow artists to obtain a richer, more luminous color than is possible with oil paint. It has been suggested that Cassatt emulated Edgar Degas's pastel technique. Rather than simply drawing with pastels, Degas manipulated them further by blowing steam onto the marked surface and working the resulting paste or wash with brushes. By the 1890s he mixed his pastels with fixative in order to superimpose layers of strokes. (Breeskin, *Oils, Pastels, Watercolors, and Drawings,* p. 17).

In the highly modeled areas of this portrait, the face and the collar, for example, Cassatt seems to have worked the pigment in several superimposed layers as if it were oil paint. In the peripheral areas, on the other hand, such as the hat's plume and the fur collar, she has used a rapidly executed gesture to denote form. Thus, this work embodies an interesting tension between description and suggestion, finish and process, similar perhaps to the contrast between the areas of roughly carved stone left by Michelangelo on all his sculptures and their otherwise highly polished surfaces.

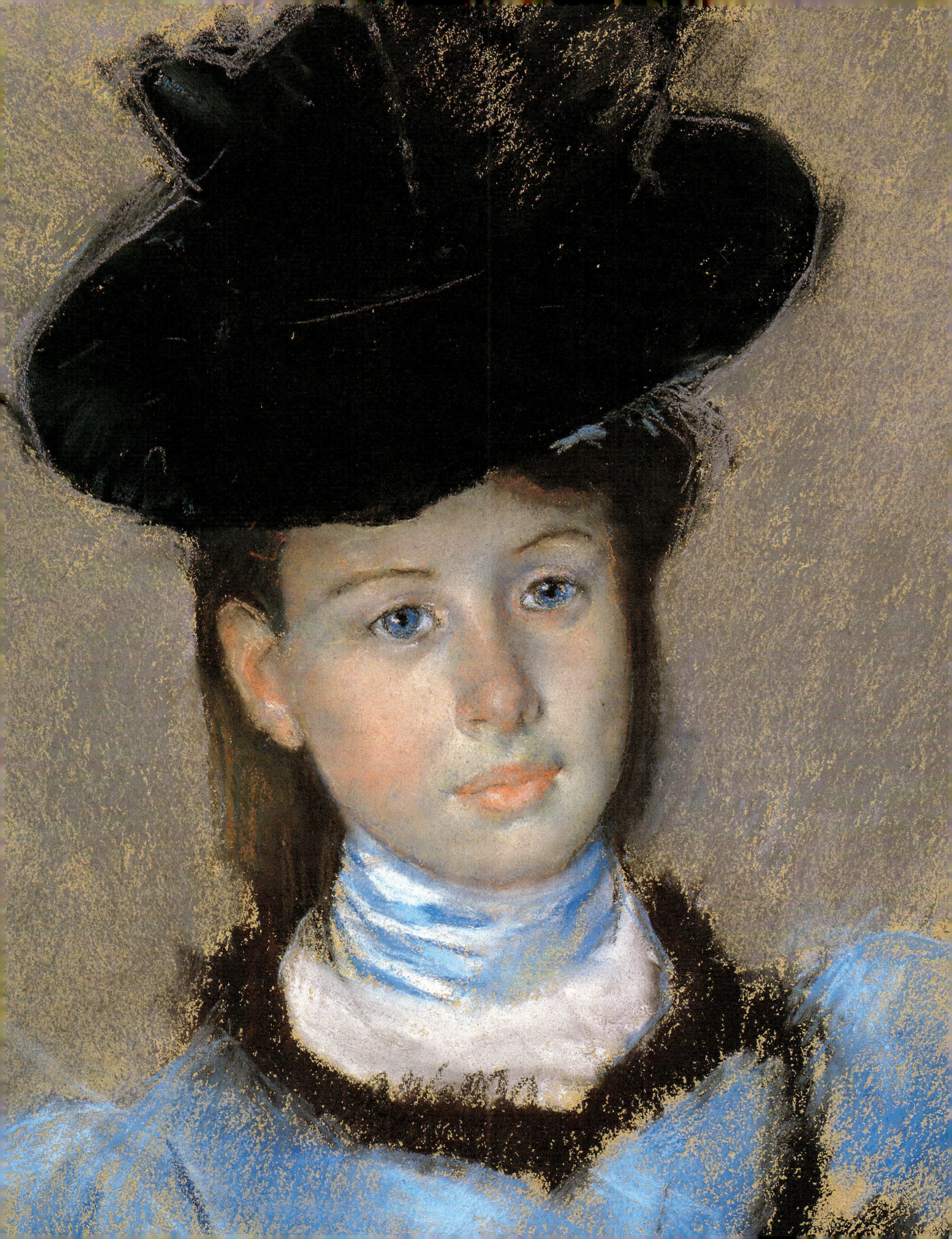

10

The Fitting

(Mathews and Shapiro 1989 9 vii/vii)
1890/1891

Color drypoint and aquatint
0.479 × 0.308 m (18⅞ × 12⅛ in.)
Chester Dale Collection 1963.10.252

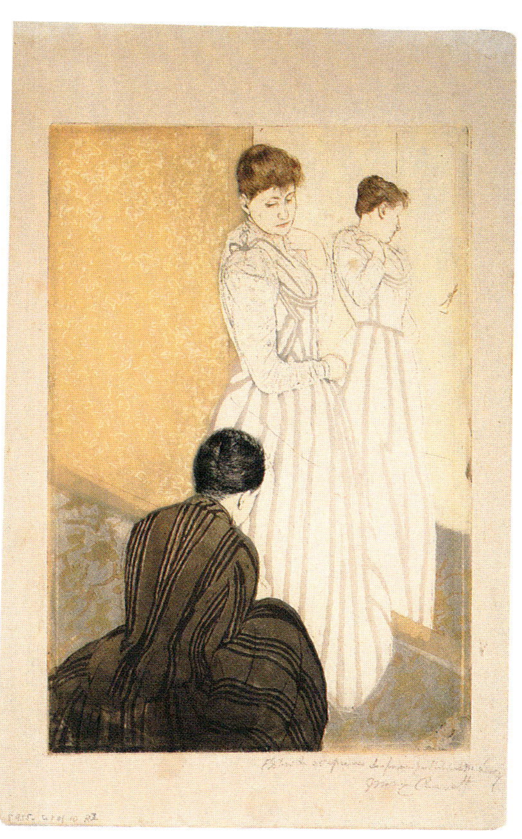

The subject of this work, dressmaking and trying on clothes, received frequent treatment in prints of the Japanese *ukiyo-e* tradition and it is easy to see how Cassatt would find such a theme compatible with her own interest in the private lives of women within the domestic sphere. Likewise, its composition, with its oblique angle and upward tilt is derived from the spatial structure of Japanese woodcuts. The background is divided into two roughly equal areas, and the main figure stands at their intersection, virtually in the center of the picture surface. The head of the seamstress is on the same axis as that of the standing figure and the two women read as a single form. Cassatt often used the mirror as an active compositional device. Here the standing figure's reflection is used to create a dynamic counter-thrust to her turning motion as she looks down over her right shoulder at the seamstress. The figure and reflection seem to be joined at the skirt and to pull apart at her shoulder.

Like many of Cassatt's works this print explores the relationship between two women, and it is typical that they are united into a single shape. The relationship here, however, contains some ambiguous elements. Despite their formal unity, a hierarchy based on social class seems to be established by the discrepancy between the figures' heights and, more important, by the fact that the profile of the kneeling seamstress is virtually hidden, allowing us to see only her back.

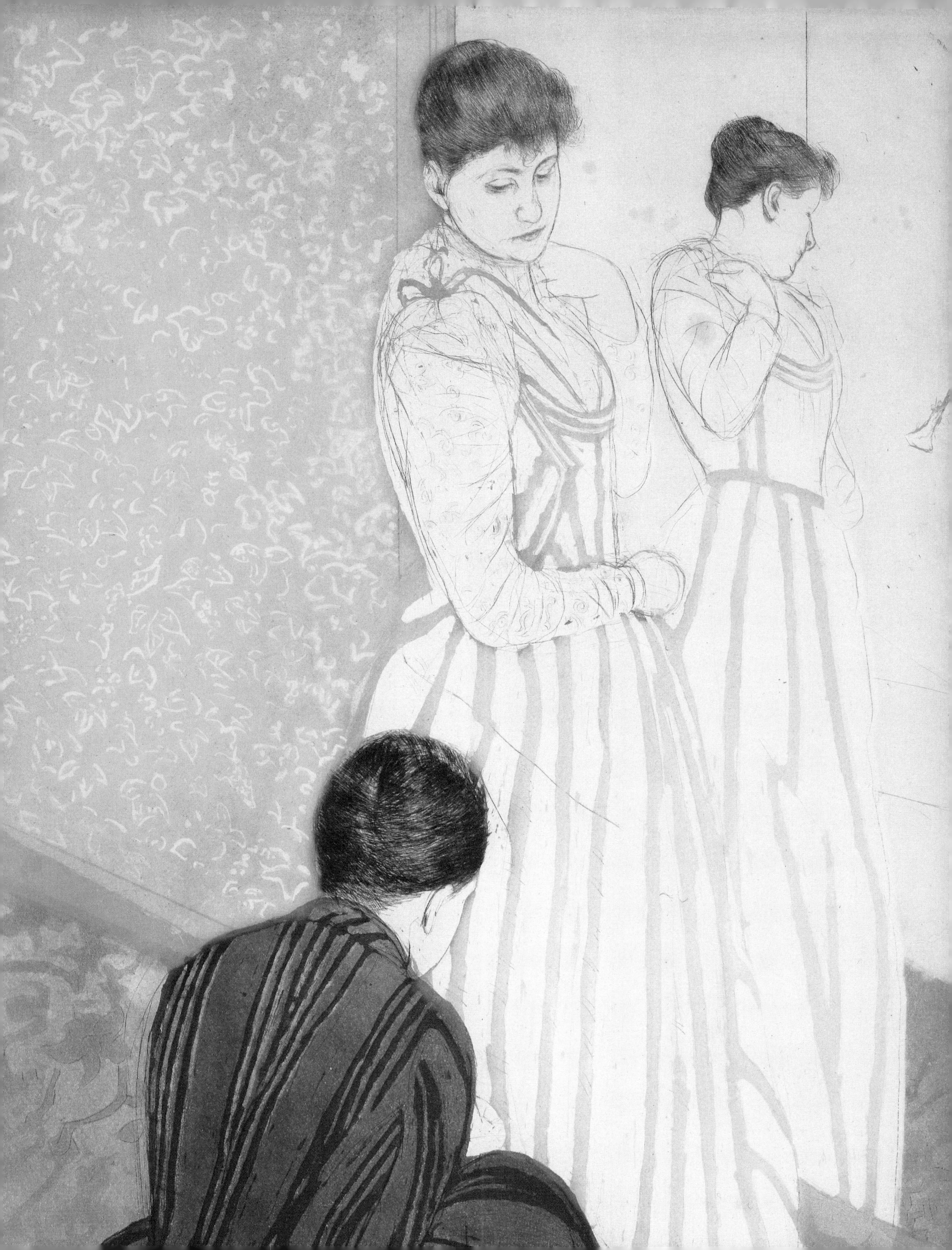

11

Woman Bathing

(Mathews and Shapiro 1989 10 iv/iv)
1890/1891

Color drypoint and aquatint
0.434 × 0.303 m (17 1/16 × 11 15/16 in.)
Chester Dale Collection 1963.10.253

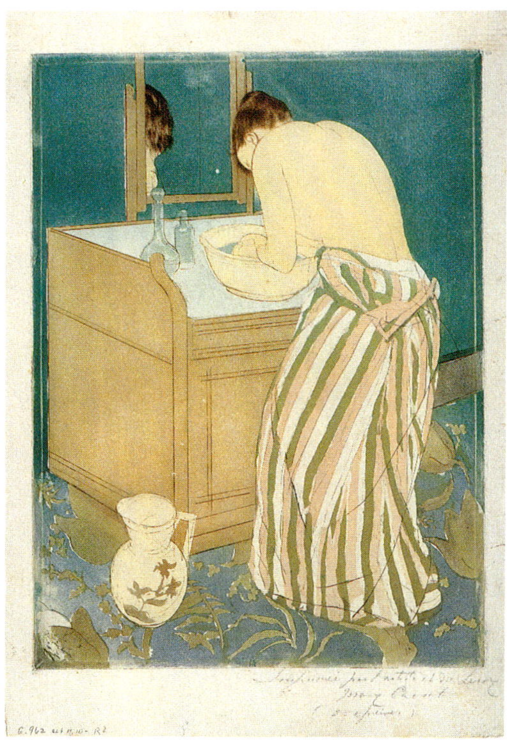

Along with *The Coiffure* (Plate 18), this is a rare example of Cassatt's use of even partial nudity in any of her mature works. For both prints, from the same series, it is likely that Cassatt chose to depict her subject in a state of semi-*deshabillé* in order to more convincingly reproduce the effects of the *ukiyo-e* prints from which they take their inspiration. In Japanese woodcuts it would not be unusual for a view of a woman bathing to reveal parts of her body usually kept hidden from public view. For Cassatt, too, the falling robe signifies the private nature of the woman's activity.

Comparison of the preparatory studies for *The Coiffure* with the final print reveal the extent to which Cassatt distilled her observations of formal volumes and specific details into abstract contour lines. Although no known studies exist for *Woman Bathing,* Cassatt's use of expressive linear abstraction is even more dramatically compelling here. The figure of a woman bent over a washbasin, seen from the back, dominates the picture surface. The sweeping curve of her shoulders is carried down through her back and buttocks, and is further accentuated by the opposing direction of the stripes of her robe as it falls over her knees, effectively communicating the figure's action of quickly splashing her face and body. Just the tiniest hint of volume is suggested by the well-placed lines denoting the indentation of her spine at the small of her back and at her shoulders.

As in her other works in this series of color prints, Cassatt revels in the use of contrasting patterns—the stripes of the robe and the flowers of the rug—which, along with the oblique perspective help to flatten the image. Her use of deeply resonant blue tones, so typical of Japanese woodcuts, is also notable.

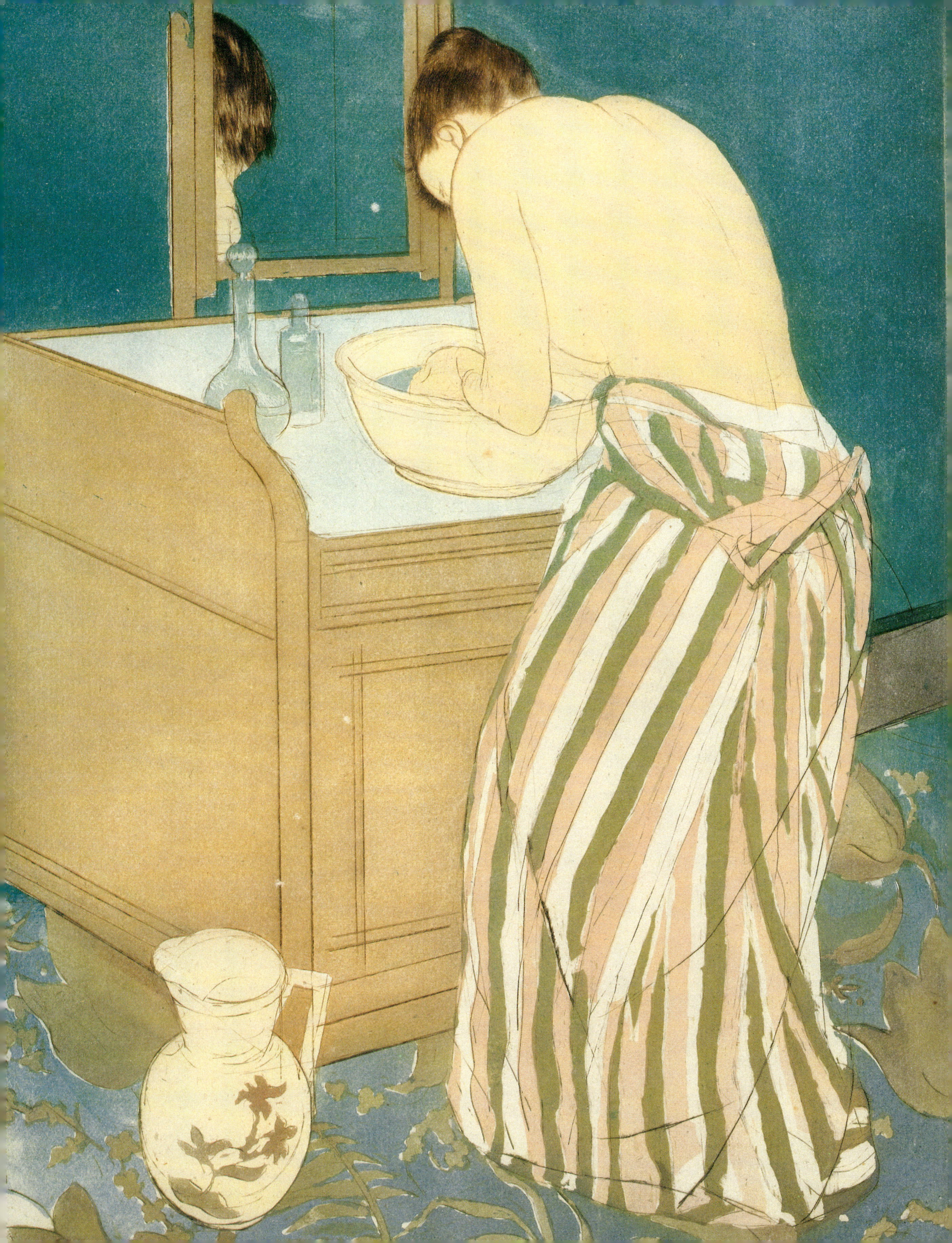

12

Woman with a Red Zinnia

1891

Canvas
0.736 × 0.603 m (29 × 23¾ in.)
Chester Dale Collection 1963.10.99

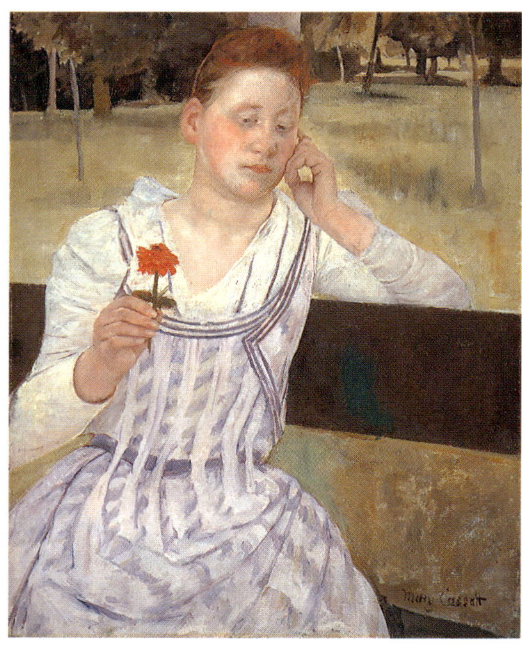

This painting is typical of Cassatt's style as it developed in the 1890s, when she was searching for a more solid means of pictorial construction. Cassatt's approach to Impressionism had never been to dissolve form, perhaps because of her early studies at the Pennsylvania Academy of the Fine Arts and of the Spanish masters. Yet, like fellow-Impressionist Pierre-Auguste Renoir, she imbued the figures in her later works with greater plastic volume than earlier examples from her oeuvre. For Cassatt, this change seems to have grown from a reassertion of her interest in the broad, solid volumes—and perhaps the allegorical significance—of Renaissance fresco painting, an influence as well on her early education as an artist.

In its precise rendering and careful modeling, this work resembles another painting of the same year, *Young Women Picking Fruit.* There are, in fact, several other noteworthy similarities. In both paintings, Cassatt has taken great care in depicting the details of the clothing, in this case the blue trim on the woman's dress. The model here bears a striking similarity to the reddish-haired standing figure in *Picking Fruit.* Finally, both works belong to a group of paintings and pastels in which Cassatt places either a solitary figure or a figural group in a landscape setting. In such paintings as *Two Women Reading* (1902), *Family Group Reading* (1901), and primarily her mural *Modern Woman,* for the 1893 World's Columbian Exposition in Chicago, as well as in this work, Cassatt contrasts a distant view of the landscape with a close-up of its inhabitants and their interactions.

Although the theme of a solitary, contemplative female figure is not unusual in Cassatt's oeuvre, the young woman's enigmatic gesture and facial expression have invited viewers to speculate concerning the nature of her thoughts.

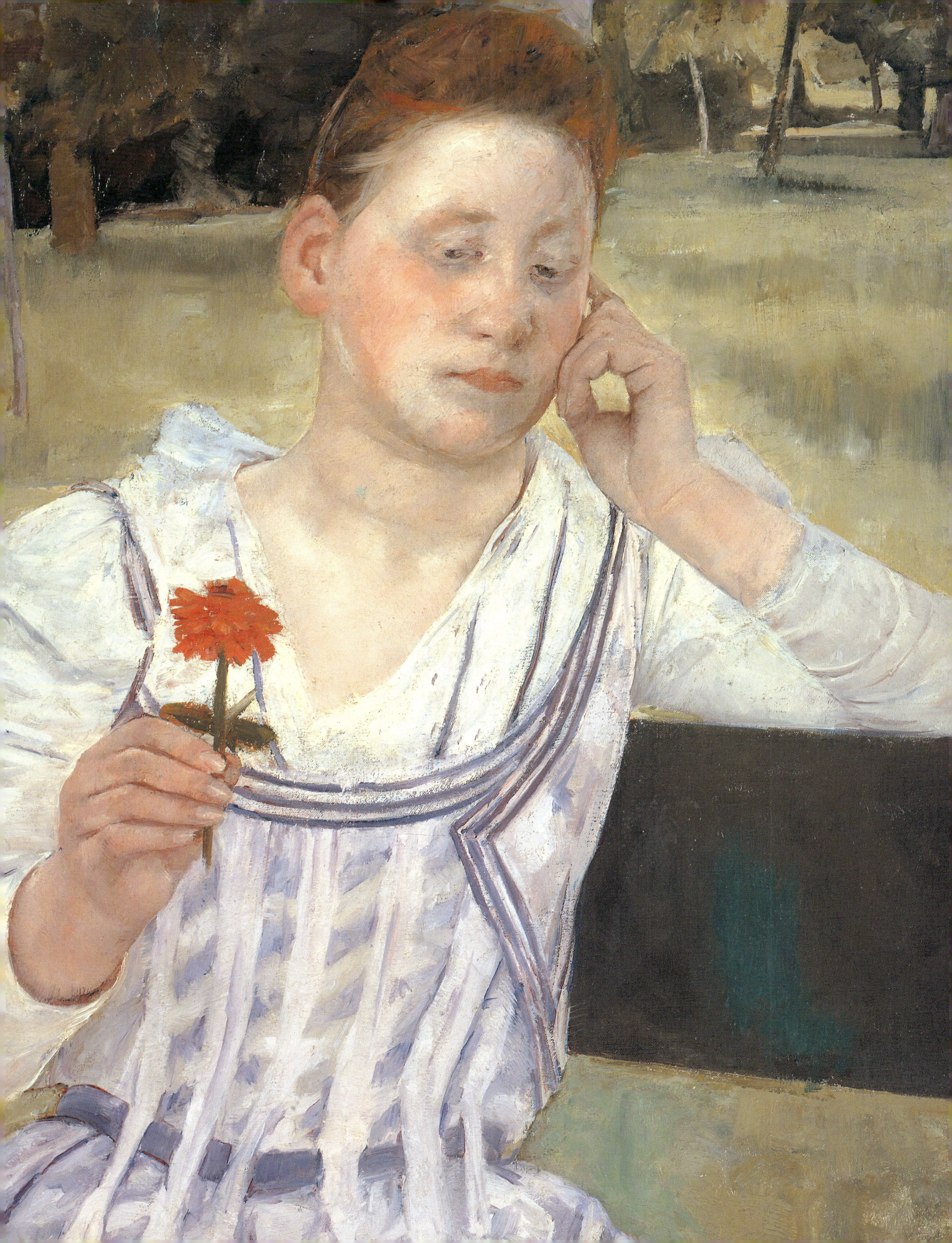

THE LETTER

(MATHEWS AND SHAPIRO 1989 8 IV/IV)
c. 1891

Drypoint, soft-ground etching, and aquatint in color
0.438 × 0.303 m (17¼ × 11¹³⁄₁₆ in.)
Chester Dale Collection 1963.10.251

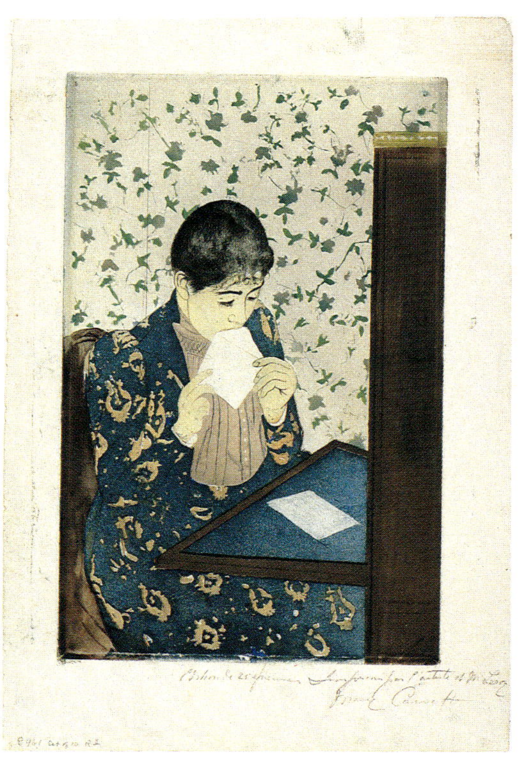

"You remember the effects you strove for at Eragny? Well Miss Cassatt has realized just such effects, and admirably: the tone even, subtle, delicate, without stains on seams: adorable blues, fresh rose. . ." Thus did Camille Pissarro convey to his son Lucien his excitement at seeing the series of color prints made by Cassatt in response to the 1890 exhibition of Japanese prints at the École des Beaux-Arts. In many ways *The Letter* is the most outstanding of that group in capturing the flavor of *japonisme.*

Perhaps the work's most striking similarity to Japanese prints lies in its shallow, compressed, two-dimensional construction of space. Cassatt uses several devices to keep the viewer's eye hovering on the surface plane—the dark vertical bar formed by the side of the desk on the right-hand border, the cropping of the chair and its position in the lower left-hand corner, the oblique trapezoidal shape of the writing surface, and the contrasting floral patterns of the background and the woman's dress. Additionally, in this work Cassatt achieved an especially vivid, lush blue (as Pissarro recognized), one that approximates the deep, translucent blue of some Japanese woodcuts. Even the features of the woman have been suggestively orientalized.

The motif and its articulation is also reminiscent of *ukiyo-e* prints, many of which depict women in the process of reading and writing letters. The gesture, too, can be found in works by Japanese masters, although Cassatt used the image of a figure with covered mouth in such earlier works as *The Loge* (1882, Plate 30), where a figure hides her face behind her fan, and *Five O'Clock Tea* (1880), in which a woman holds a cup of tea to her mouth.

The subject of a woman alone, caught in a private moment, is typical of both Japanese prints and Cassatt's oeuvre.

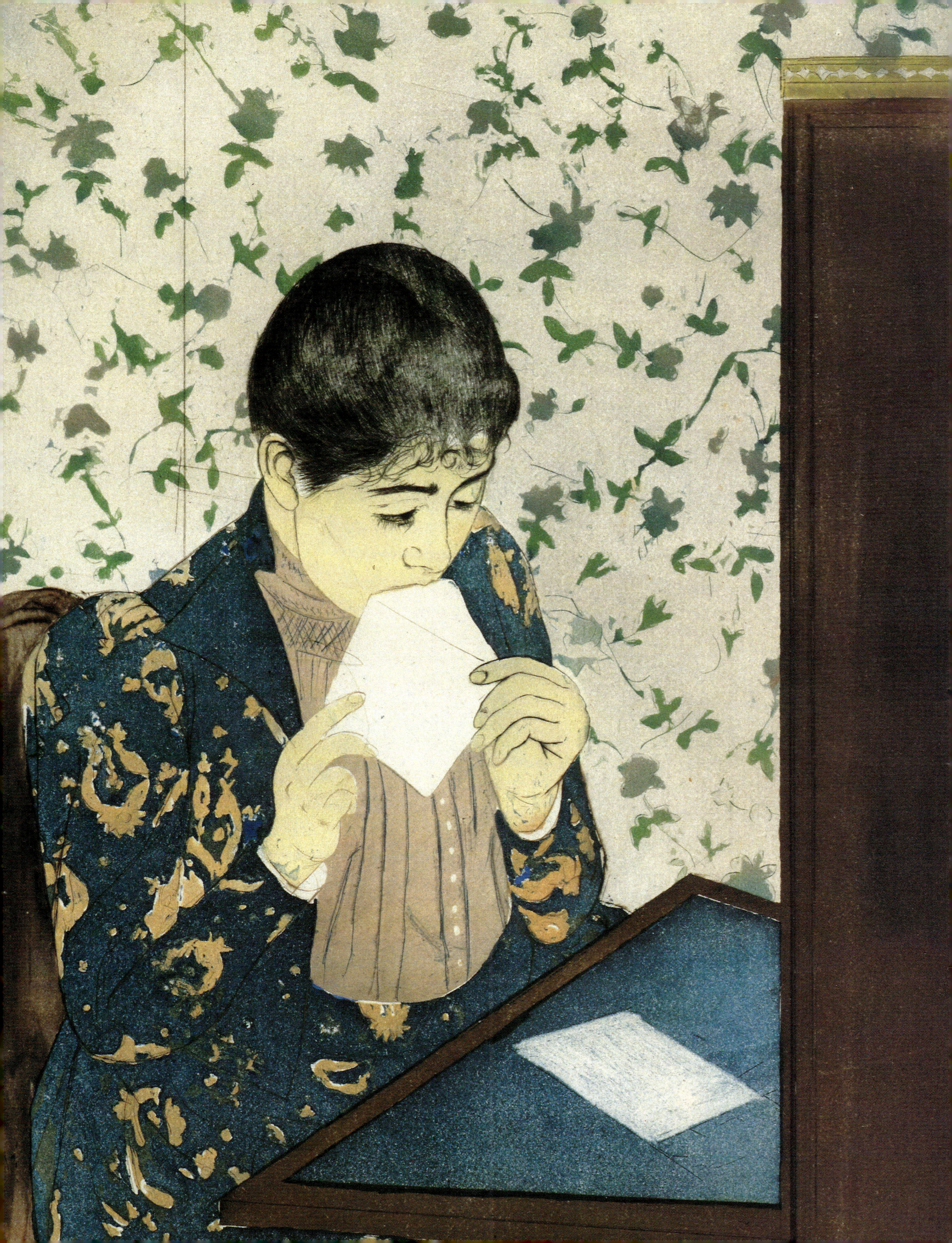

14

Maternal Caress

(Mathews and Shapiro 1989 12 vi/vi [proof B])
c. 1891

Drypoint and soft-ground etching in color
0.427 × 0.312 m (16 13/16 × 12 5/16 in.)
Rosenwald Collection 1943.3.2761

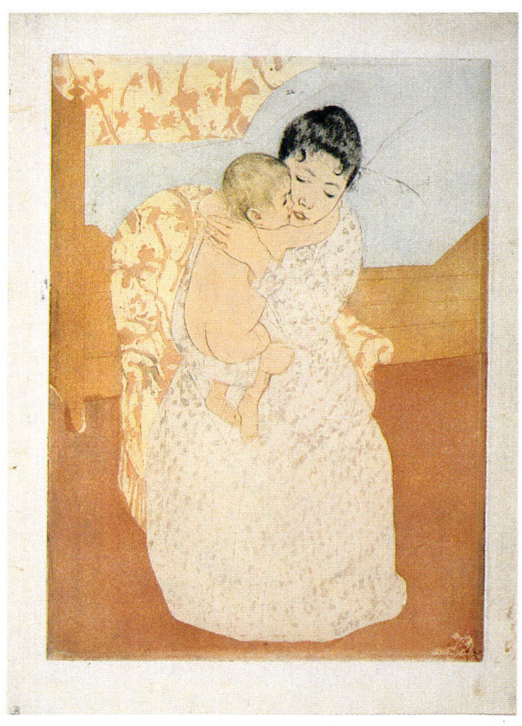

One of the series of ten color prints inspired by her viewing of the 1890 École des Beaux-Arts exhibition of Japanese woodcuts, this work shows Cassatt's increasing interest in exploring mother-child interactions. The centrally placed figures, locked in a tight embrace, dominate the entire picture surface, not only its foreground.

Cassatt has used several pictorial devices to emphasize the close relationship between mother and child. The most effective is that the two read as a single unit, the child inscribed within the shape of its mother. The contour of the mother's right arm as it holds the child is reflected by the curve of the baby's back and buttocks, which helps to accentuate their formal unity. Similarly, the contours of their hugging arms form two ellipses that pivot around their closely-placed faces. The baby burrows his face into his mother's; the mother's eyes are closed as if in ecstasy.

Cassatt has also taken pains to emphasize the solidity of their combined form. Together they create a pyramid whose base is the outline of the mother's dress. Cassatt extends the unit's mass and the space that it occupies by integrating the figures with the chair on which they sit. Not only does the baby become one with the mother, but they both merge with the contours of the chair. The resultant increase in visual weight further accentuates the sense of stability and, as such, the image is reminiscent of ancient representations of maternal strength in which women's procreative power was linked to the concept of a throne or seat.

The space of this intimate interaction is clearly a private one, although Cassatt did not add the bed until the second state. Except for a small amount of black used for the outlines and the mother's hair, the colors are remarkably delicate in tone: lavender, gray, pale yellow.

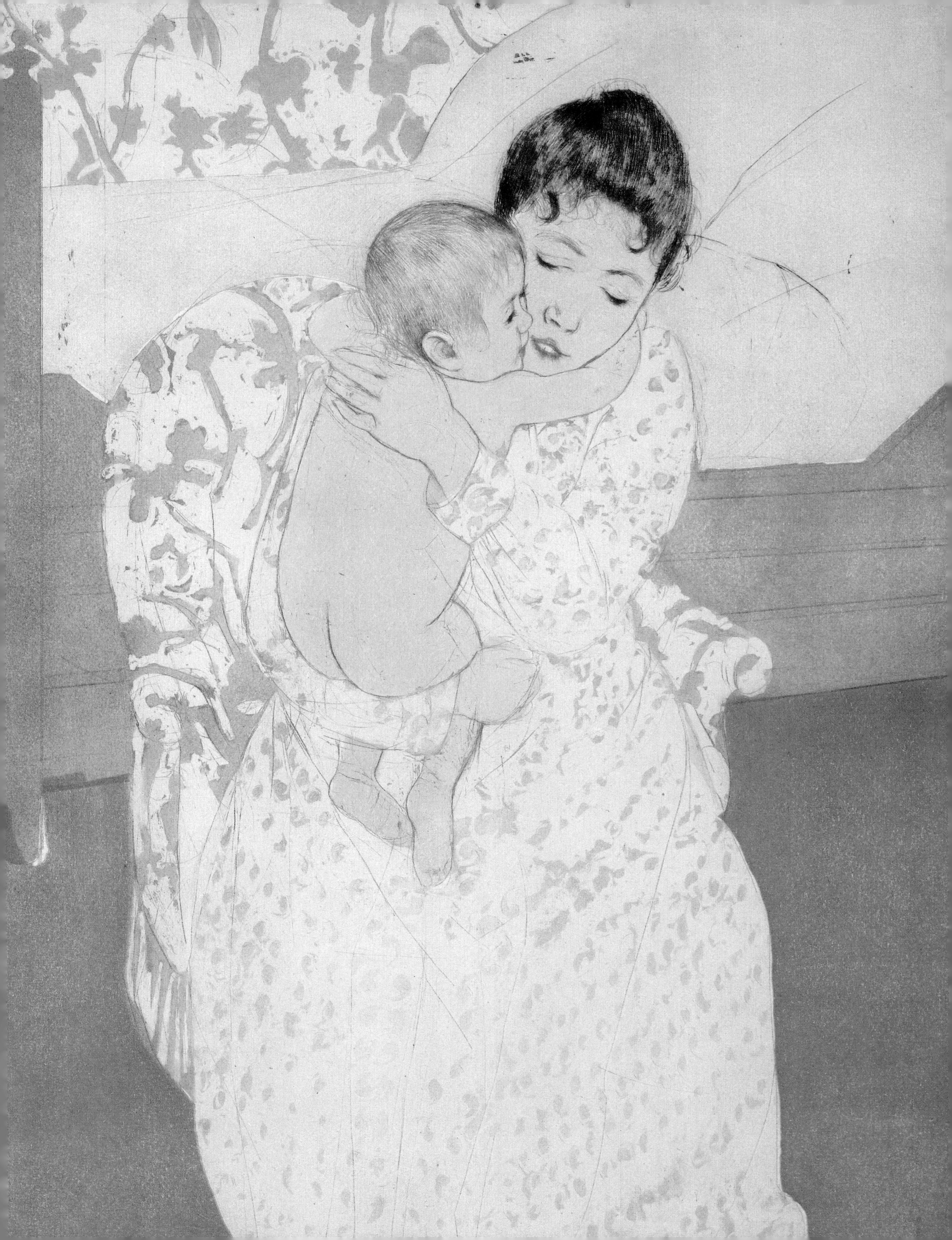

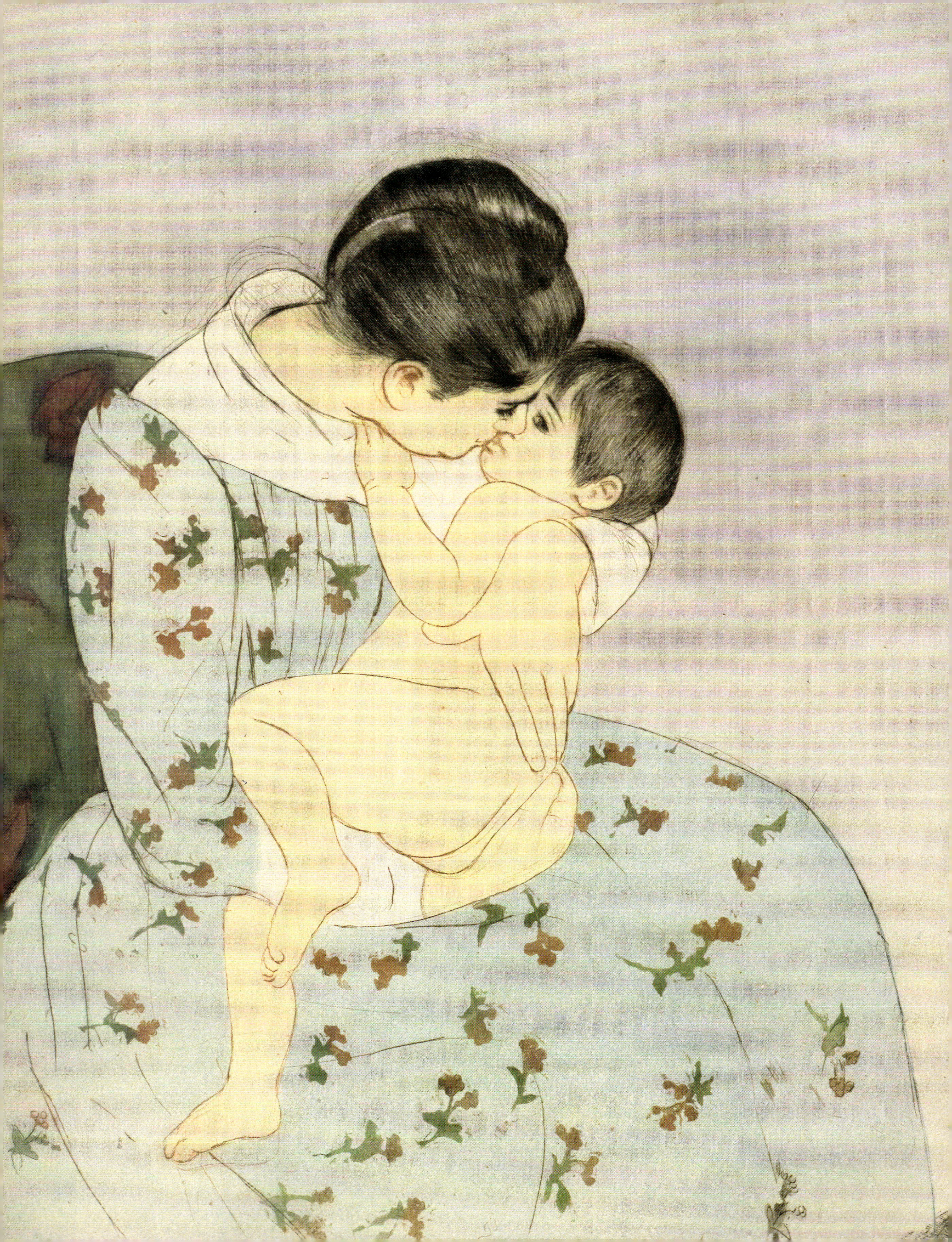

15

MOTHER'S KISS

(MATHEWS AND SHAPIRO 1989 II V/V)
c. 1891

Drypoint and soft-ground etching in color
0.434 × 0.302 m ($17^{1}/_{16}$ × $11^{7}/_{8}$ in.)
Chester Dale Collection 1963.10.254

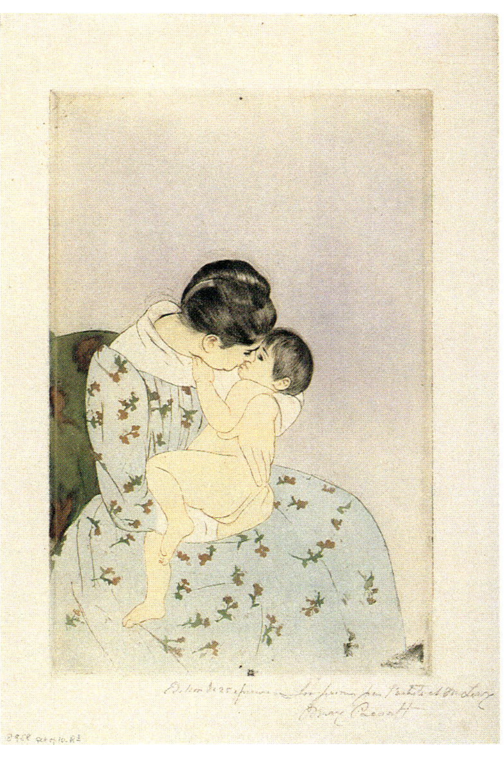

This color print explores the subject of the bond between mother and child, a theme in which Cassatt continued to become increasingly interested. Here, she uses several of her favorite compositional devices to communicate to the viewer their close relationship. Cassatt melds the child and its mother into a single form by establishing a series of continuous and reflexive contours at the point of their embrace. The contour of the mother's right arm is reflected by that formed by the connection of her hand with the child's back, and the fore-arm with which she cradles his buttocks is reiterated by the shape of his thigh above it. Together, these lines and forms create a circular rhythm that binds the figures together.

As in many other of Cassatt's works, the figures are joined at the face and brow so that the contours of their heads and their hairlines read as a single form. In this work Cassatt has taken this device a step farther, by connecting and overlapping their features. We see only one eye and eyebrow of each figure; likewise, the mother's nose overlaps and hides that of her baby, while we see the baby's lips but not the mother's.

For all their closeness, however, there seems to be some opposition between these figures. The baby glances back out at the viewer, raising its eyebrow with a troubled look, suggesting that perhaps he is resisting his mother's kiss. The gestures of his hand at her neck and his knee under her breast might well suggest that he is pushing her away, rather than clinging to her.

Cassatt has not made any attempt at suggesting the details of the spatial setting inhabited by these figures. By concentrating the entire mass in the lower left-hand corner, and balancing it with the negative space of the background, Cassatt gives even greater visual weight to the dyad of mother and child.

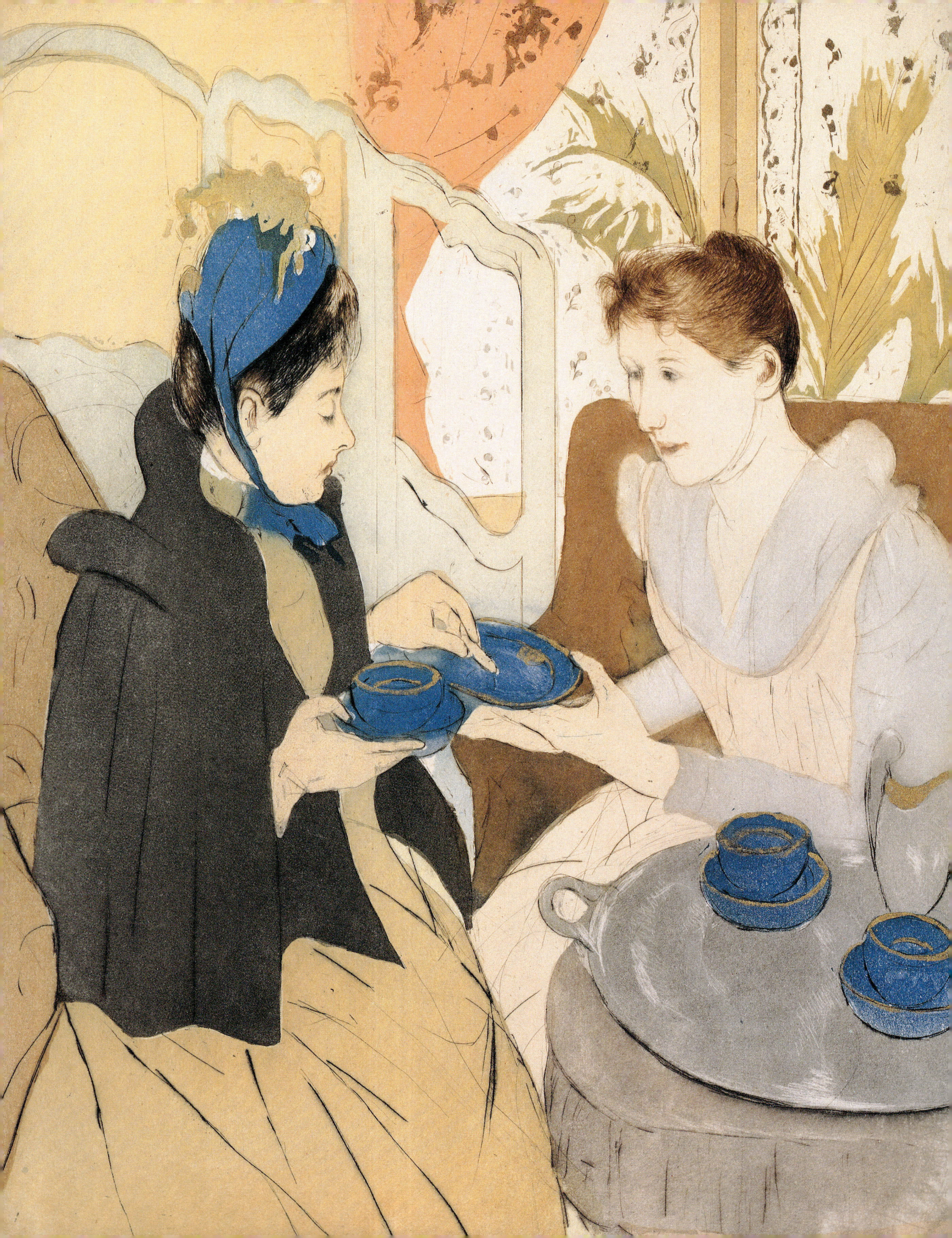

16

Afternoon Tea Party

(Mathews and Shapiro 1989 13 v/v)
c. 1891

Color drypoint and aquatint on laid paper
0.425 × 0.311 m (16¾ × 12¼ in.)
Chester Dale Collection 1963.10.256

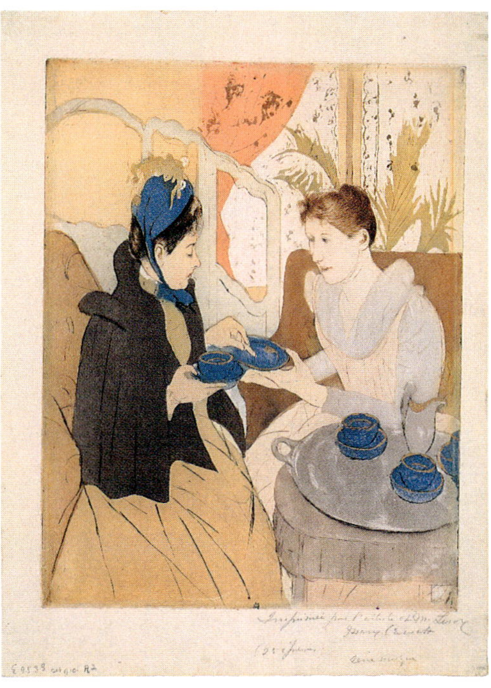

"Statues and articles of *vertu* filled the corners, the whole being lighted by a great antique hanging lamp. We sipped our *chocolat* from superior china, served on an India waiter upon an embroidered cloth. . . ." Thus May Alcott Nieriker, sister of author Louisa May Alcott and the model for Amy in *Little Women,* described "tea at Miss Cassatt's" to her mother Abigail May Alcott in November 1876. At that time, Nieriker was a young American woman studying art in Paris; Cassatt, at thirty-four, was famous for giving elegant teas in her well-appointed living quarters.

Cassatt also favored teatime as an artistic subject, exploring it in both paintings and graphic works. This print is reminiscent of one of her most noted works on the theme, *Five O'Clock Tea* (1880), in which her sister Lydia entertains a guest over a large silver tea service which occupies the lower right-hand corner of the picture surface. The tea set holds the same prominent position in this work as well; here, however, the right-hand figure is shown offering some morsels of food from a plate to her guest, who balances her cup and saucer in one hand. The china depicted here, deep blue with a gold rim, is similar to that featured in Cassatt's *Lady at the Tea Table* (1883–85), a portrait of Mrs. Robert Moore Riddle, Cassatt's mother's cousin.

The ritual of taking tea was a quintessential part of the nineteenth-century *haut-bourgeois* woman's world to which Cassatt belonged, in which women were proud to display their domestic treasures to the admiring eyes of other women. Additionally, teatime provided an opportunity to pursue the warmth and intimacy that characterized many relationships between women in the late nineteenth century.

17

The Bath

(Mathews and Shapiro 1989 5 xvi/xvii [proof X])
c. 1891

Drypoint and soft-ground etching in
yellow, blue, black, and sanguine
0.376 × 0.276 m (14⅜ × 10⅞ in.)
Rosenwald Collection 1943.3.2760

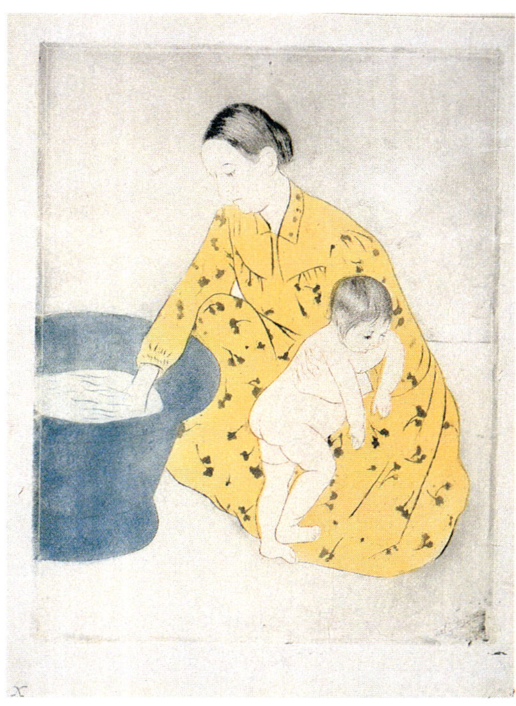

In this print of a mother reaching into a tub of water with her right hand to bathe the squirmy, naked child that she holds with her left, Cassatt comes remarkably close to recreating the ambience of the Japanese woodcuts that were her inspiration for a series of ten prints of which this was the first. The theme itself is one that was common to prints in the *ukiyo-e* tradition (seen in works by such artists as Toyokuni and Utamaro), that showed the daily concerns of the residents of the Edo (Tokyo) pleasure district, whose domestic activities often included caring for their children.

The bathing routine figured in a number of Cassatt's works in various media. Her earliest use of this theme, *Mother About to Wash Her Sleepy Child* (1880), is usually considered to be her first major painting exploring the mother-child relationship. In that work, as in this print, Cassatt reveals her keen eye for capturing characteristic gesture, as the sleepy child seems to resist its mother's ministrations. The theme is explored again in her later painting, like the print also titled *The Bath* (1892), in which a mother and an older child both focus their gazes on the child's feet soaking in a tub. When compared to the 1880 work, the Japanese influence on this later painting—with its severely oblique spatial construction and flattening contrast of pattern—is quite pronounced.

The print, however, shows its lineage even more directly than either painting. Cassatt has eliminated all distracting background details from this work, to allow the viewer to focus on the interaction between mother and child, communicated through subtle characteristic gestures, such as the way the child grabs the mother's kimono and presses his foot down on her knee. As in *The Letter* (Plate 13), Cassatt has orientalized the features of both figures.

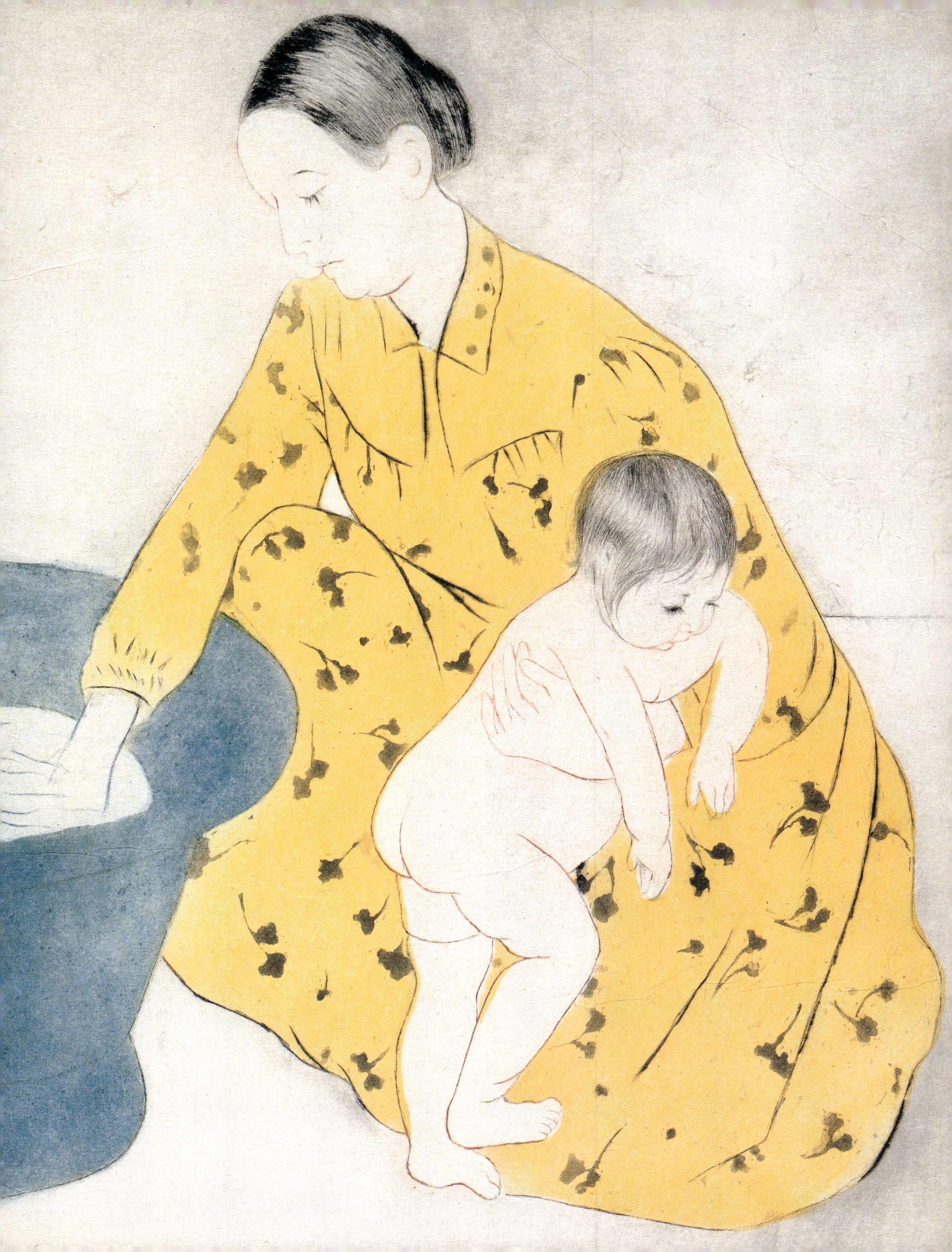

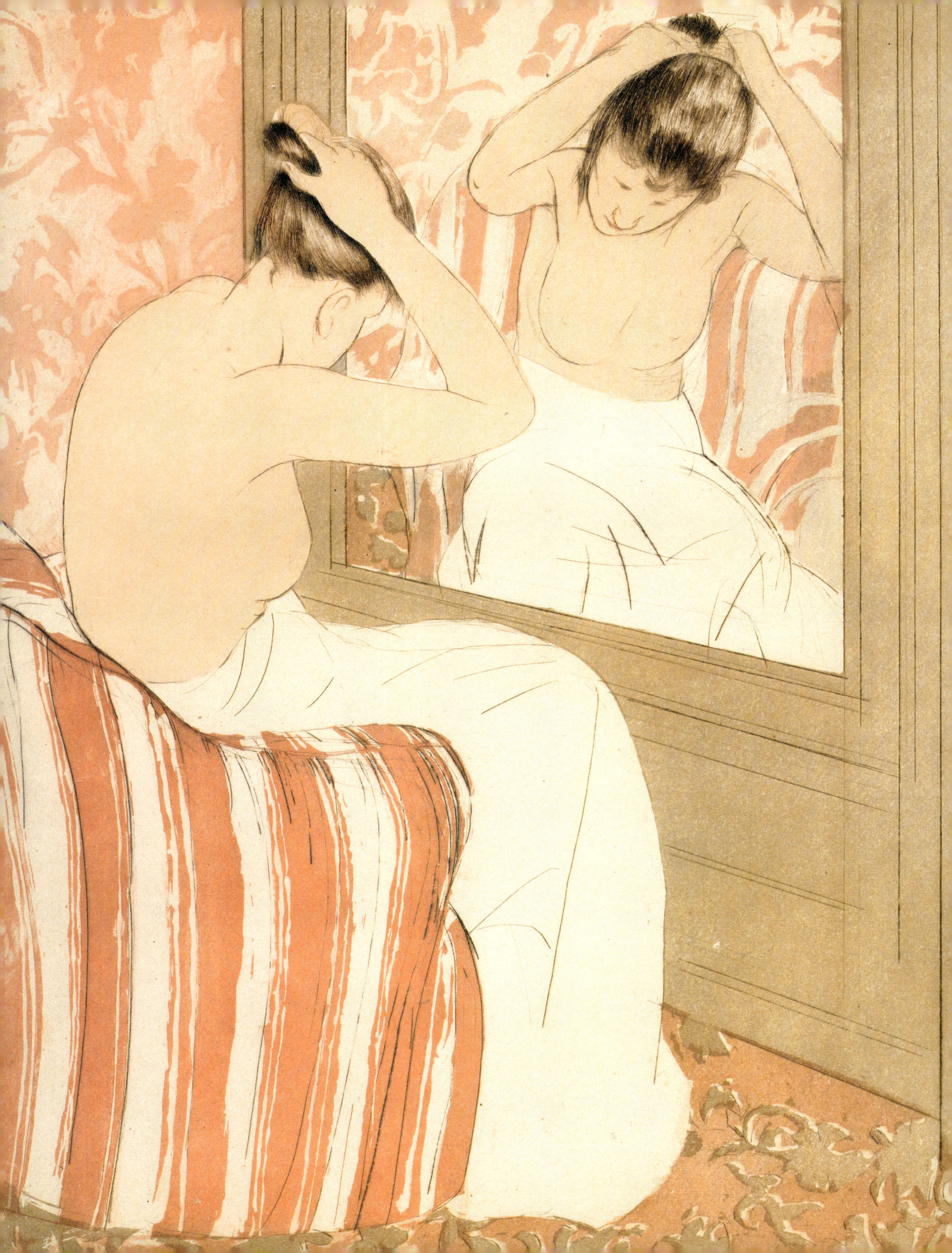

18

The Coiffure

(Mathews and Shapiro 1989 14 v/v)
c. 1891

Drypoint and soft-ground etching in color
0.432 × 0.307 m (17 × 12¼ in.)
Chester Dale Collection 1963.10.257

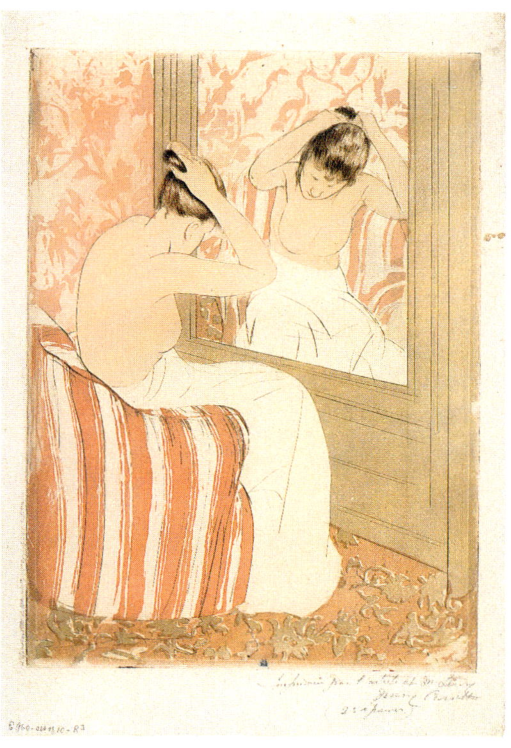

Tenth in the series of ten color prints inspired by Cassatt's viewing of the 1890 École des Beaux-Arts exhibition of Japanese woodcuts, this work's subject is especially related to the *ukiyo-e* tradition in which intimate scenes of bathing and dressing were often depicted. Actually, Cassatt used a similar theme in her 1886 painting of a *Girl Arranging Her Hair* (Plate 6), well before she saw the Japanese exhibition, and her Impressionist colleague, Berthe Morisot, also used the motif of hair-coiffing in her own works. Many of *The Coiffure's* pictorial elements are typical of Cassatt's oeuvre: the play on a mirror and its reflections, the obliquely inclined composition, and the contrasting, flattening patterns, such as the flowers in the rug and wall and stripes on the chair.

On the other hand, the figure's partial nudity is quite atypical of other works by Cassatt. Adult nudity occurs in only one other late work, *Woman Bathing* (1890/1891, Plate 11), from the same series, where we see the figure's naked back, but not a full image of the breasts, as is visible here. It is likely that the figure's nudity can be explained as an attempt to emulate its prototype more closely. *Ukiyo-e* artists such as Utamaro and Toyokuni often showed bare breasts in their glimpses into the domestic lives of the residents of the Edo Yoshiwara (Tokyo pleasure district). Unlike the western tradition's display of the female nude for a male gaze, the intimate detail in both the Japanese prints and in Cassatt's work is fleeting, and the woman is allowed the privacy of her own world, her absorption in her *toilette.* The prevalent pink tonality of this work emphasizes the self-contained and private sphere of a woman's boudoir.

19

In the Omnibus

(Mathews and Shapiro 1989 7 vii/vii)
c. 1891

Soft-ground etching, drypoint, and aquatint in color
0.432 × 0.298 m (17 × 11¾ in.)
Chester Dale Collection 1963.10.250

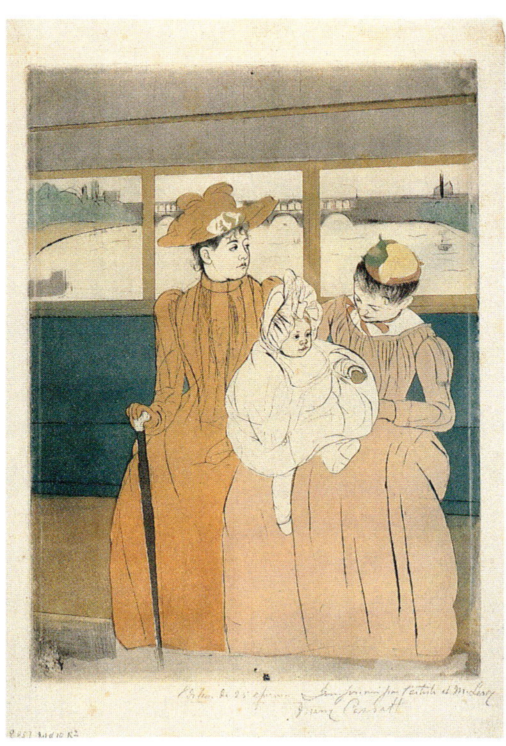

The setting of this work, a means of public transportation, suggests its link to Honoré Daumier's painted depiction of *The Third-Class Carriage* (c. 1862), a work that was owned by Cassatt's friends, the Havemeyers. Despite their many differences, both works provide a glimpse into the lives of the denizens of the modern city; as such, it was quite unusual in Cassatt's oeuvre. Although in earlier states of the print, Cassatt left the window area blank, here the city is clearly visible in the background through such details as a bridge, tall buildings, and boats on the river.

As in Daumier's painting, this work focuses on a mother, a child, and a third figure. The exact relationship among these figures, however, is somewhat ambiguous. While it is possible that the woman on the left is simply a relative or friend, and the right-hand figure is the child's mother, the contrast in their costume suggests that the right-hand figure is perhaps the child's nurse. If so, Cassatt makes here an interesting observation concerning the upper middle-class mother's role. Although the baby in Cassatt's print is visually situated between its elegantly-attired mother and the nursemaid, it is actually seated on the nursemaid's lap. Furthermore, while the maid is actively concerned with the child, the mother gazes into the distance somewhat distractedly.

Although the spatial construction of this print and its use of color are consistent with the Japanese woodcuts that were its inspiration, in its subject matter—daily life in nineteenth-century Paris—it is closer to works by Cassatt's Impressionist contemporaries.

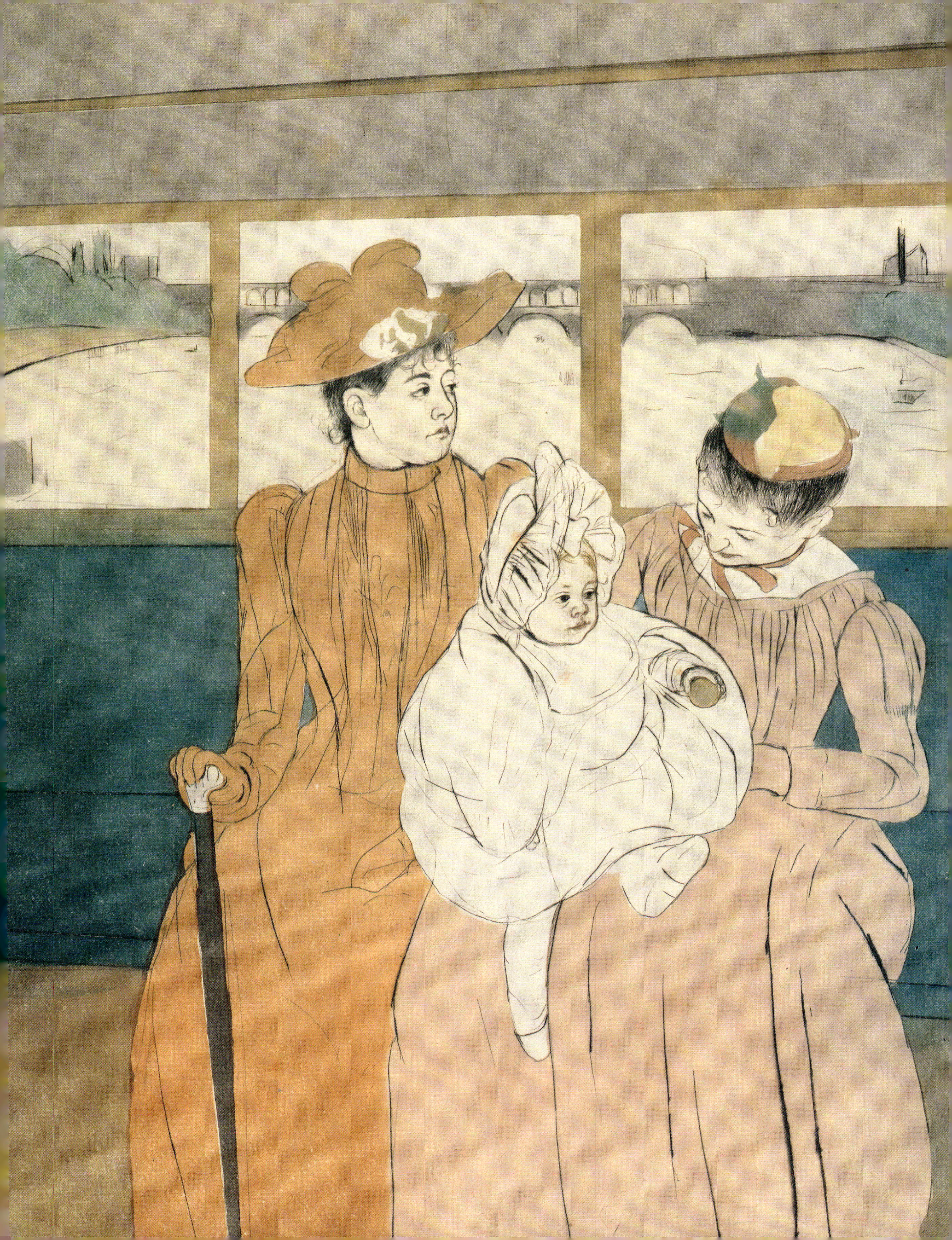

20

The Lamp

(Mathews and Shapiro 1989 6 iii/iv [proof B])
c. 1891

Drypoint, soft-ground etching, and aquatint in color
0.438 × 0.305 m (17¼ × 12 in.)
Rosenwald Collection 1943.3.2762

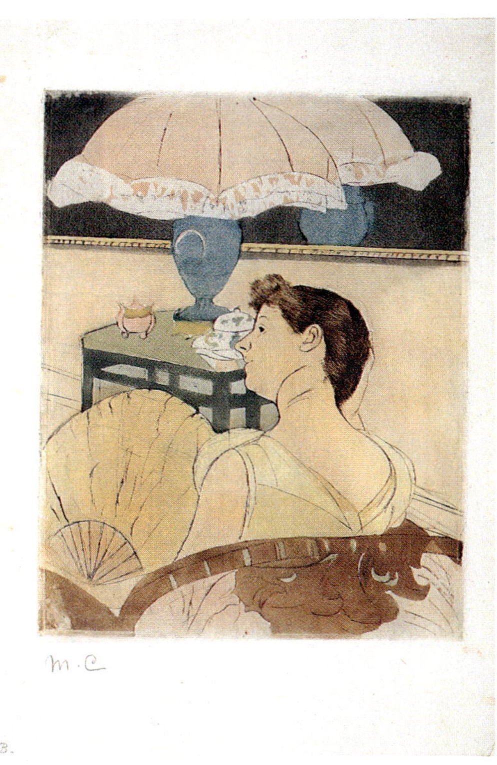

The most notable feature of this print is the unusual point of view of both artist and viewer, standing behind a couch on which a female figure is seated. Cassatt seems to have placed herself slightly to the figure's left, as if she were looking into the space of the room over her subject's left shoulder. Consequently, the back of the chair, which reads as a horizontal band almost parallel to the work's lower border, creates a visual barrier in the immediate foreground. The figure's slightly upturned face is depicted only in profile, while we concentrate on her back, centrally placed in the foreground of the print.

Another intriguing visual element of this work is the predominance of linear arabesques. The most obvious of these is the contour of the lampshade, whose scalloped edge, repeated by its reflection in a mirror, spreads across the entire upper quarter of the picture surface. This form is echoed in numerous pictorial details. It is particularly evident in the arc of the fan, and the curve of the figure's left shoulder and of the back and arm of the chair, particularly in the lower left corner. More subtly, it appears in the chair's floral pattern, the shape of the lamp as it is reflected in the mirror, the china bowl on the table, and even the figure's upturned nose and quirky smile. At about the same time that Cassatt made this work, the French artist Georges Seurat theorized that linear rhythms could be used to express emotions (arabesques implied cheerful ones). Furthermore, linear arabesques are characteristic of Japanese woodcuts, so influential to Cassatt at this time in her career.

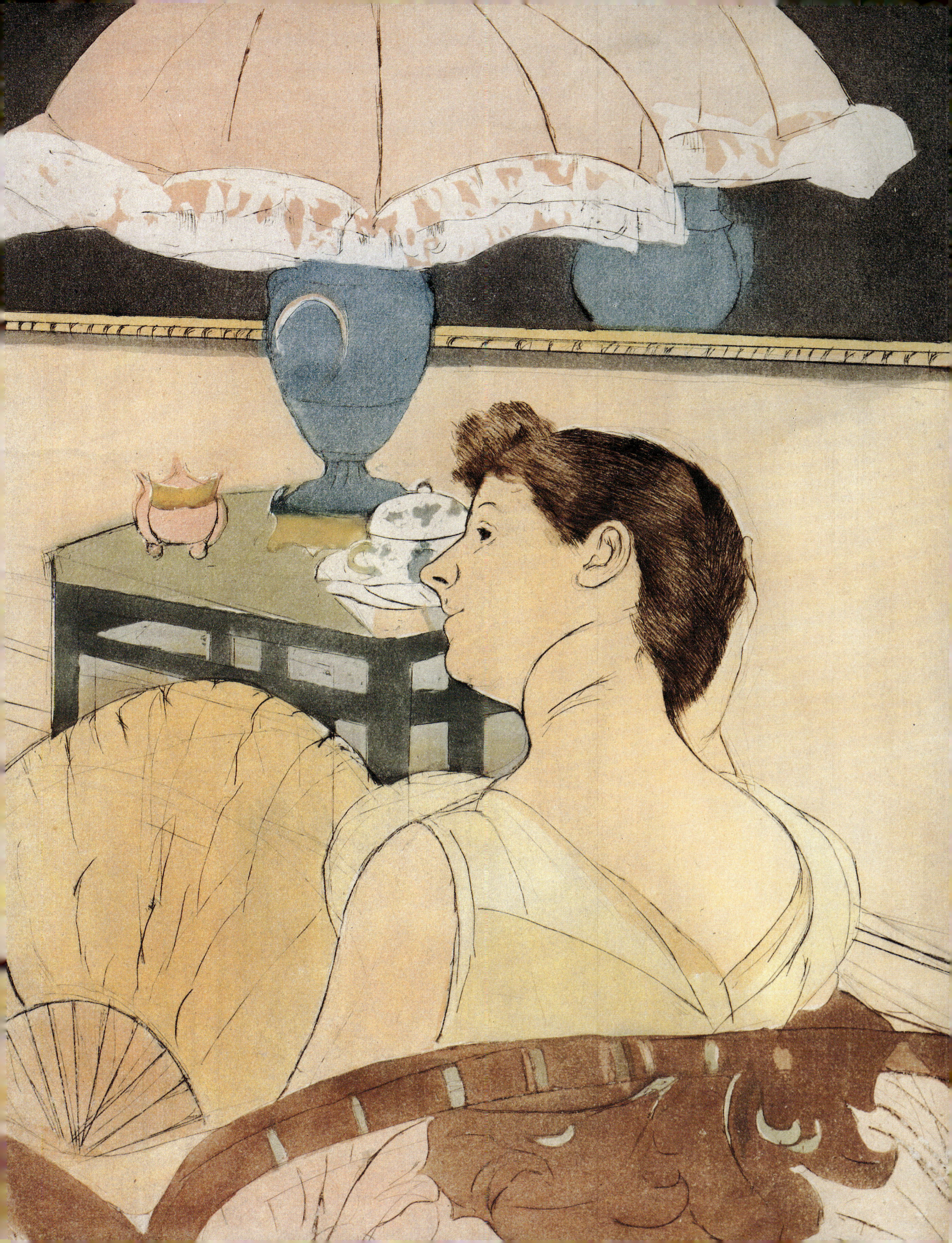

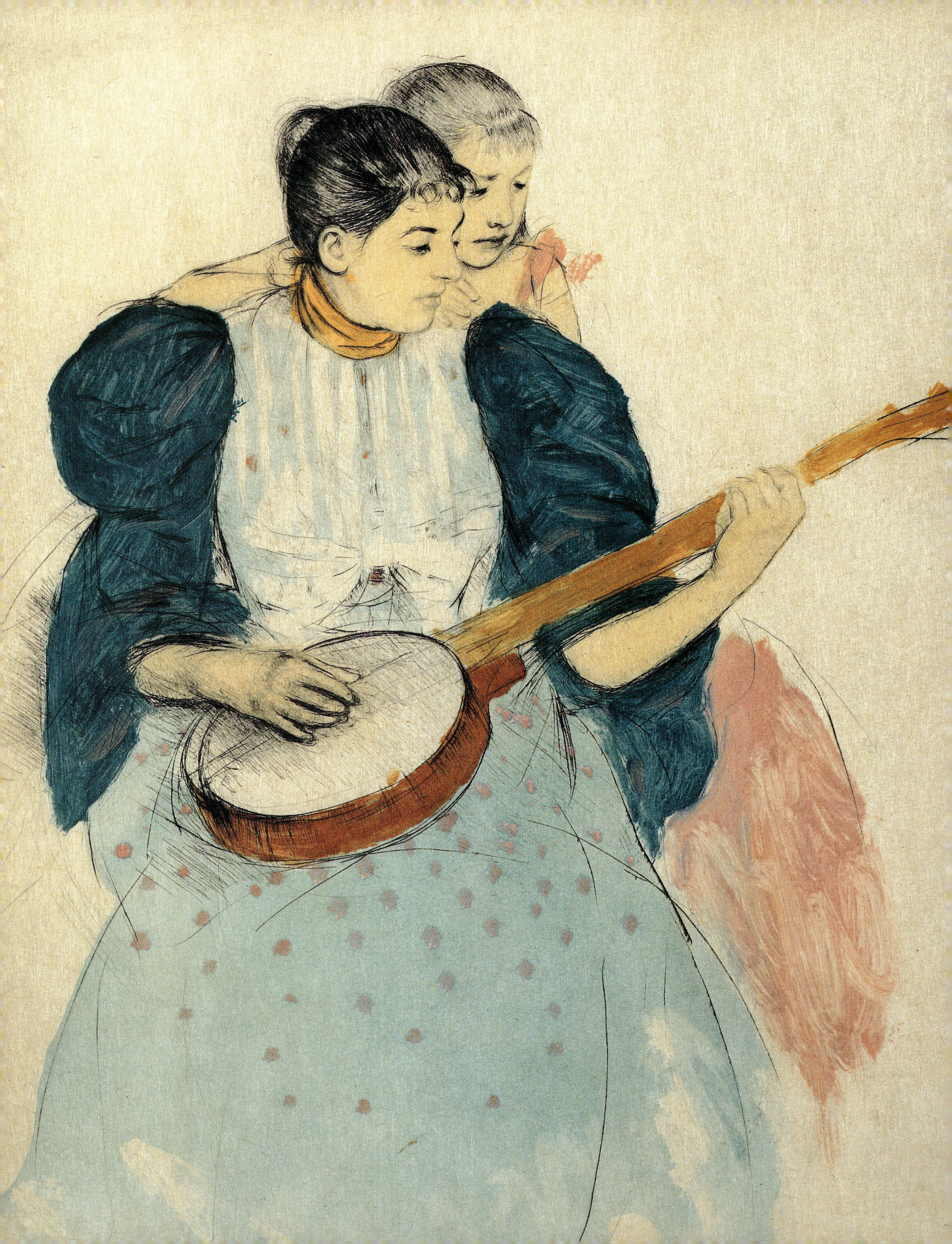

21

The Banjo Lesson

(Mathews and Shapiro 1989 16 iv/iv)
c. 1893

Drypoint and soft-ground etching in color
0.419 × 0.292 m (16½ × 11½ in.)
Gift of Mrs. Jane C. Carey as an addition to
the Addie Burr Clark Memorial Collection 1959.12.6

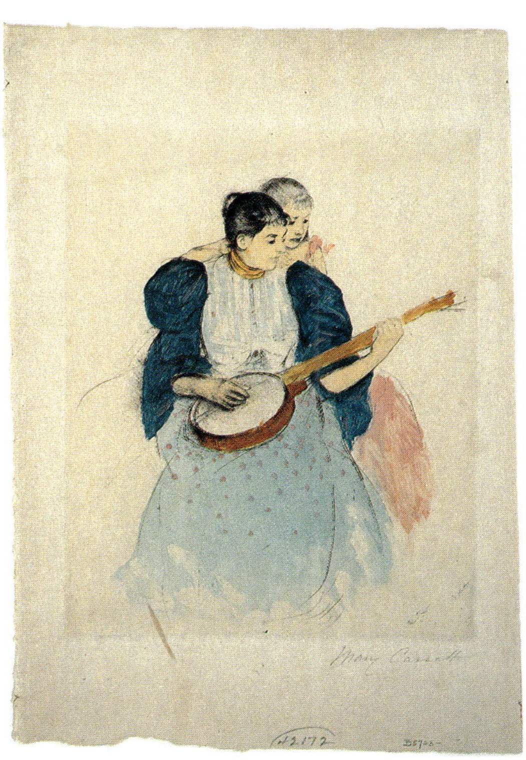

Dated several years later than her great series of ten color etchings, this work shows Cassatt further refining her skills as a printmaker. A comparison of the four states of this work reveal her method of developing her images—from lightly sketching in the principal details with drypoint, through the use of soft-ground to show tonality, and finally to the addition of color.

The subject of the work is the intimate interaction between the two figures. As in other works depicting the relationship between two women, Cassatt has used many of the same formal devices with which she elsewhere emphasizes the closeness between mother and child. The two figures read as a single shape, the upper arm of the girl seeming to grow out of the left-hand sleeve of her teacher's dress. As in so many of Cassatt's depictions of mothers and children, or of friends, their faces are placed to form a unit, and their hair and brows follow a connected contour. They both focus their attention on the same spot, another device Cassatt often used to express intimacy, in this case, the teacher's left hand on the banjo's neck. The unit's monumentality is further emphasized by the contrast of its pyramidal shape and dark tones against the stark, barely articulated background.

The same duo was the subject of a slightly later pastel (also *The Banjo Lesson,* 1894). Although that work is articulated in greater detail, it lacks the formal clarity of this print, perhaps precisely because of its greater descriptiveness.

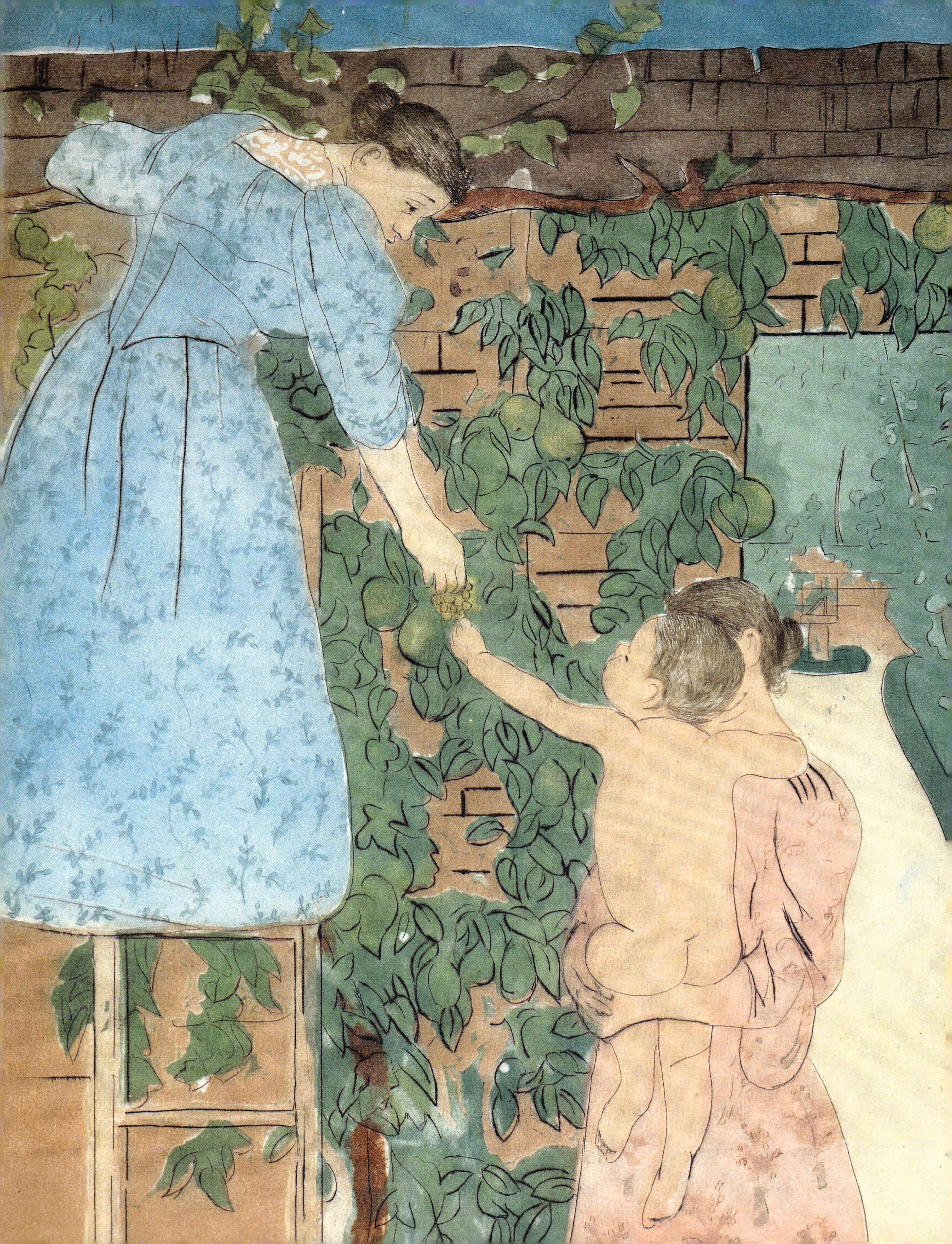

22

Gathering Fruit

(Mathews and Shapiro 1989 15 xi/xi)
c. 1893

Drypoint and aquatint in color
0.422 × 0.295 m ($16^{5}/_{8}$ × $11^{11}/_{16}$ in.)
Rosenwald Collection 1943.3.2757

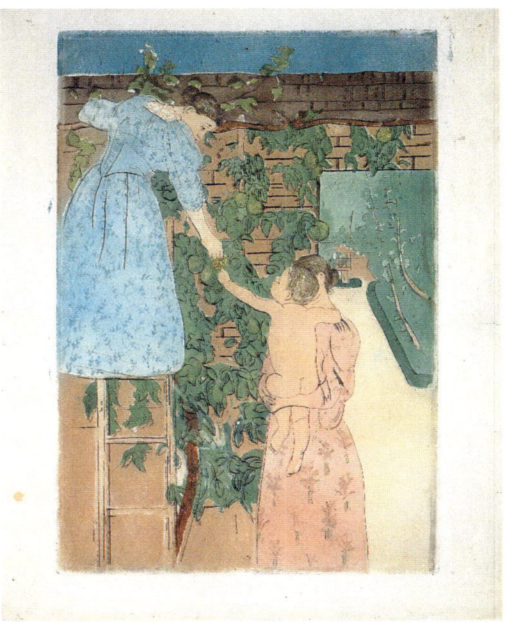

Time and subject link this print to three paintings (as well as several prints and drawings) by Cassatt, all centered around the image of fruit-picking: *Young Women Picking Fruit* (1891), *Baby Reaching for an Apple* (1893), and the mural Cassatt painted for the Chicago World's Columbian Exposition of 1893 in which she represented modern womanhood by showing *Young Women Plucking the Fruits of Knowledge and Science.* The subject of picking fruit was also depicted by Cassatt's contemporary and sister Impressionist, Berthe Morisot. Although in her mural, Cassatt imbued the theme with symbolic overtones, its use in this work, and in those by Morisot, is more simply descriptive. During the nineteenth century, picking fruit was one of the few acceptable outdoor activities for proper bourgeois women.

Here, as in her other works on the same theme, Cassatt combines gesture and direction of gaze to connect the figures. The woman on the ladder looks down at a baby to whom she offers a bunch of grapes from her downward-stretched arm. The baby, in turn, looks up at her while reaching up his arm to take the grapes. The grapes fill the space between their outstretched arms in a way that is reminiscent of the gap between God and Adam's outstretched arms on the Sistine Chapel ceiling. This visual analogy is probably not completely coincidental; Cassatt was, in fact, at this time looking back at Renaissance sources.

One curious aspect of this image is that the baby's face hides that of the person holding him. Together, the figures create a single triangular form, a device Cassatt often used to communicate the closeness of the mother-child bond. In this work, however, the relationships among the two women and the baby are not clearly delineated.

23

The Boating Party

1893/1894

Canvas
0.902 × 1.171 m (35½ × 46⅛ in.)
Chester Dale Collection 1963.10.94

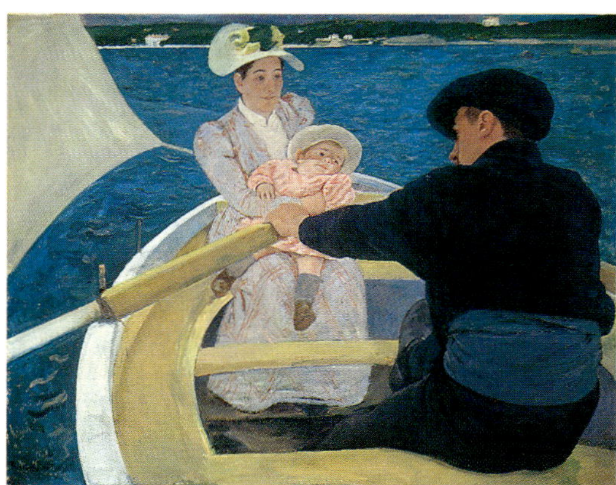

This work invites comparison with Manet's painting *Boating* (1874), purchased at Cassatt's suggestion by the Havemeyers, friends whom she advised on art collecting. Here, however, the oarsman's back is to us, whereas in Manet's work he is centrally located and makes direct eye contact with the viewer. *The Boating Party* is characterized by severe cropping, a device Cassatt used often but rarely as dramatically as here, particularly in the sail, cut off at the left-hand border, and in the tilted angle of the boat's hull. The extremely high horizon allows only the thinnest sliver of sky to show at the upper border, which helps focus our attention on the figures in the boat.

The presence of the oarsman is unusual in that men rarely entered Cassatt's works, yet here he is in a prominent position, a looming dark shape that dominates the foreground. The expression on the mother's face is somewhat distracted and anxious. Although it has been suggested that her concern could indicate some tension with the oarsman, more likely it is in response to the baby who struggles against her tight grip as she attempts to hold him in a rather precarious position.

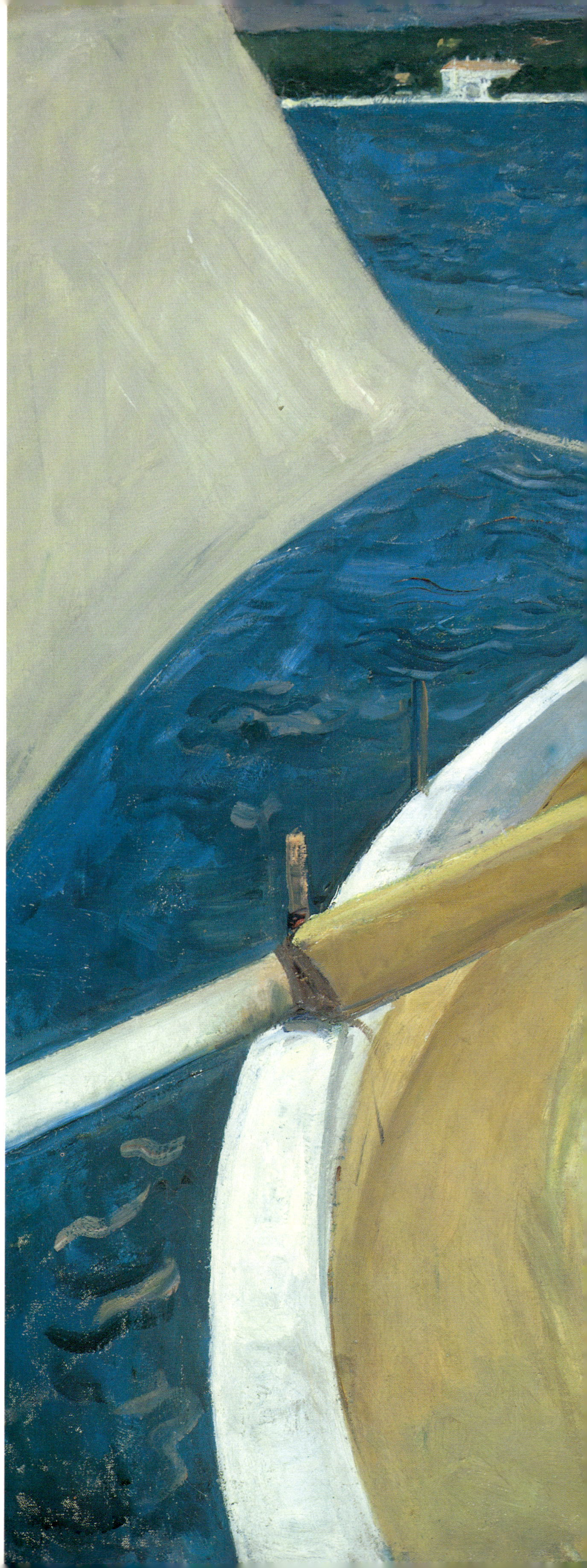

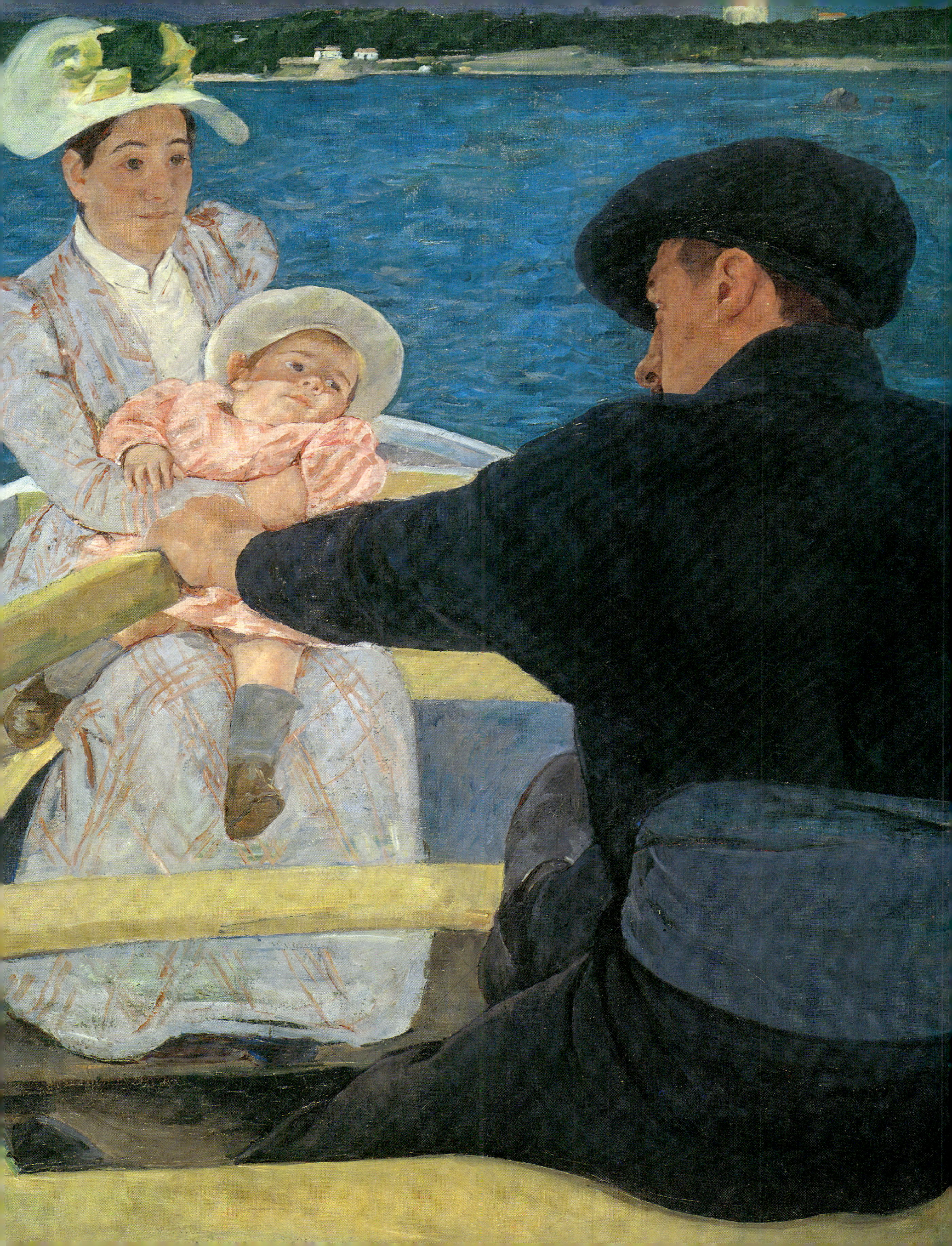

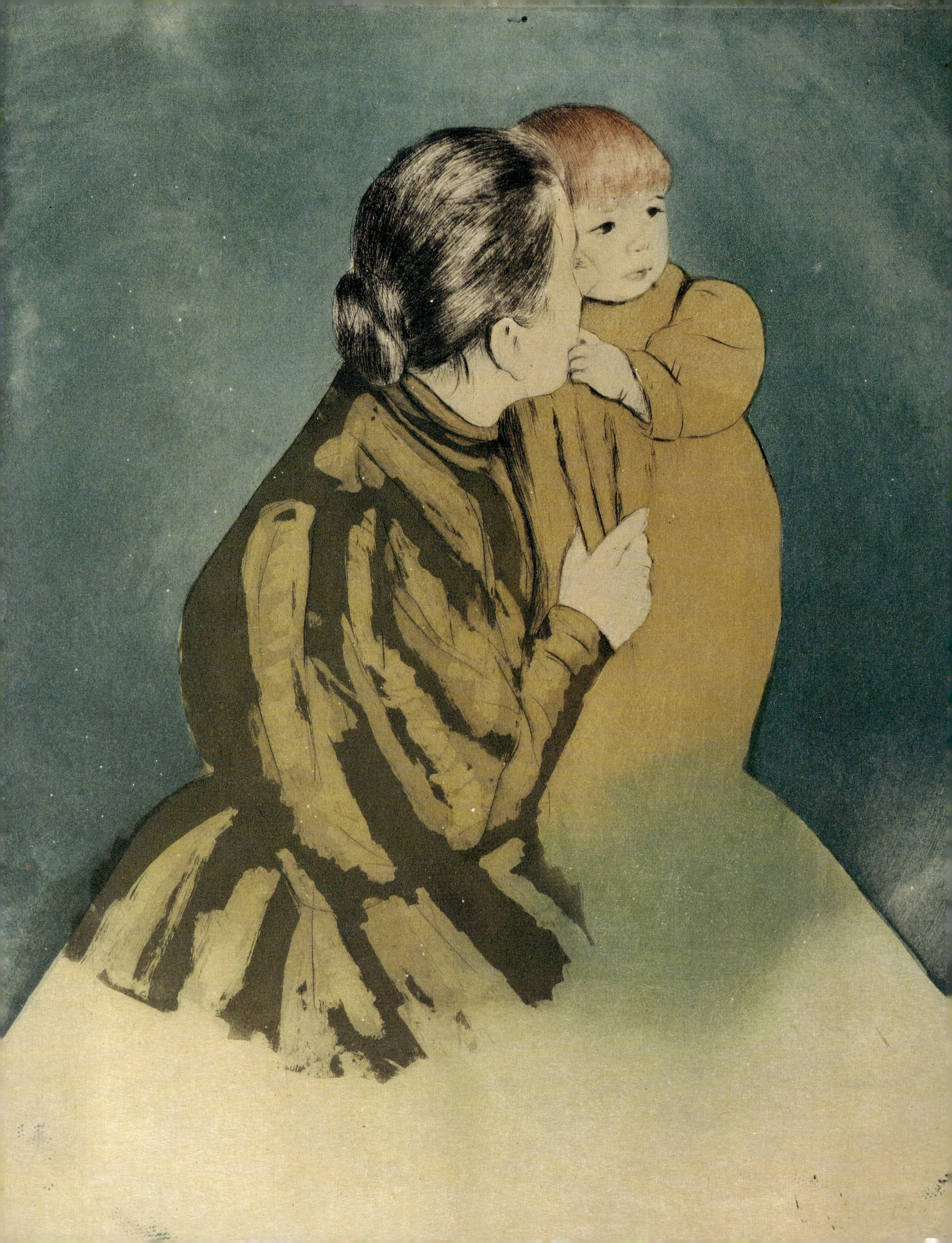

24

Peasant Mother and Child

(Mathews and Shapiro 1989, 17 ix/x [proof E])
c. 1894

Drypoint and aquatint in color
0.467 × 0.292 m (18⅜ × 11½ in.)
Rosenwald Collection 1943.3.2749

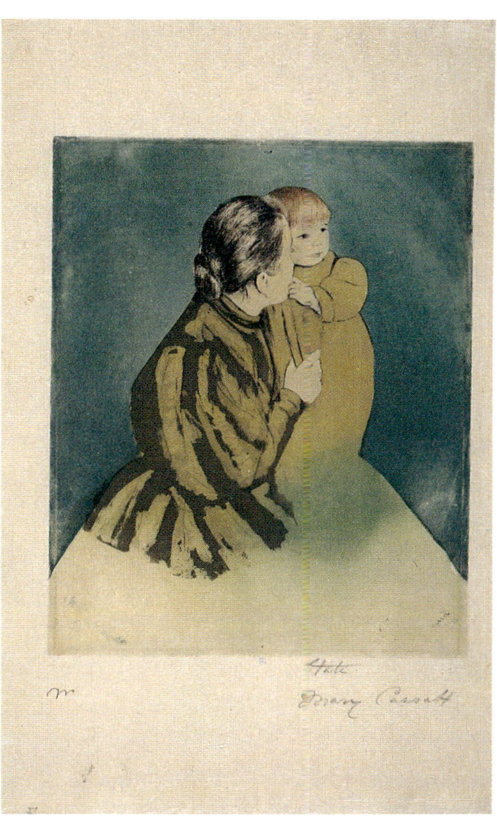

As Cassatt became increasingly interested in the *maternité* theme, she gravitated toward depicting less-affluent mothers who tended their children themselves, rather than relegating their care to nursemaids. In these relationships, she perceived greater intimacy in the attachment between mother and child.

The print is built of large shapes with a limited palette, and virtually no background detail. Together, the mother and child form a pyramid whose top is created by their joined heads and whose base, the mother's skirt, extends along the entire lower border. The unit of their bodies creates a very solid and stable form.

The focal point of the work is established in the center of the composition, however, where Cassatt creates visual weight through greater differentiation in pattern and color—the stripes in the mother's dress and the ocher of the baby's outfit. The joined figures establish an elliptical rhythmic flow, the focus of their interaction, which is further emphasized by the reflexive nature of their contours and by the pattern formed by their connecting arms. In this work, as in others from the same time, the mother's face is hidden by her baby's, except for the very tip of her nose. As in so many other evocations of the intimacy of the maternal dyad, Cassatt connects these figures at the line of their brows.

Notwithstanding the timeless, universal quality of this work, Cassatt shows herself a keen observer of specific gestures. Here, the mother steadies the child by holding the folds of its garment, and the child connects with its mother by sticking its fingers into her mouth.

25

Under the Horse-Chestnut Tree

(Mathews and Shapiro 1989 20 III/III)
c. 1895

Drypoint and aquatint in color
0.410 × 0.290 m (16³⁄₁₆ × 11⁷⁄₁₆ in.)
Gift of Mrs. Jane C. Carey as an addition to
the Addie Burr Clark Memorial Collection 1959.12.4

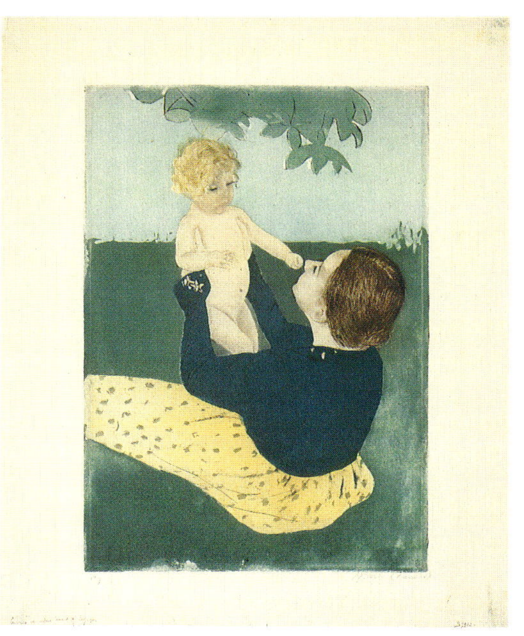

In this work, the latest of her prints included in this volume, Cassatt investigates some of the artistic concerns that typify her oeuvre during the last decade of the nineteenth century. This print is similar to other works in several media from the 1890s in which she places a close-up figure or group of figures in a landscape setting. A grassy park expands around this mother and her child who dominate the foreground, and the relatively high horizon helps focus our attention on their activity. The leaves barely outlined against the sky at the work's upper border are the only hint of the chestnut tree of the title. The same dark-haired mother and blond curly-headed child are probably the subjects of another print, *By the Pond* (c.1898), also a close-up view of a mother and child out-of-doors.

The theme, the infinitely varied interactions that comprise the relationships between mothers and their children, had become especially important to Cassatt by this time. She shows these figures gazing tenderly at each other as the mother balances her standing baby on her stomach or thighs. As always, Cassatt carefully records the specific gesture, including here the pressure of the mother's thumbs at the baby's armpits, the spread fingers of the baby's right hand, and the little fist as it reaches out for the mother to kiss.

Cassatt at this time also liked to experiment with unusual perspectives. As in her slightly earlier print, *The Lamp* (c. 1891, Plate 20), in this work the artist and viewer are positioned behind the main figure, and her back is in the immediate foreground, allowing us to see her face in partial profile only. This placement, and the acute foreshortening of her image, creates the effect that the viewer, like the mother, is gazing up at the baby. When coupled with the grassy expanse and the high horizon, they communicate the sensation of being down on the ground, playing with the baby and seeing the world from its point of view—or perhaps from that of its mother.

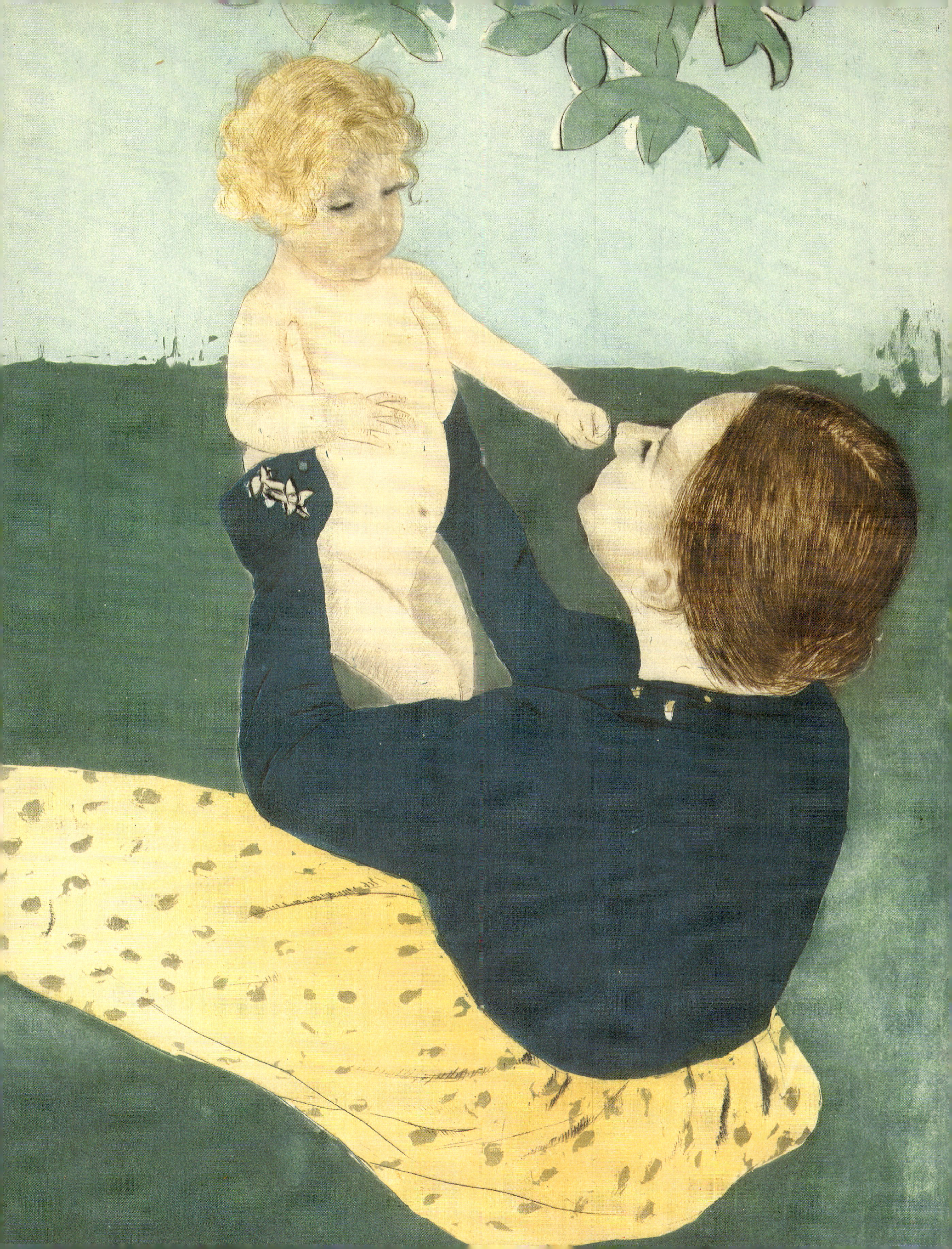

26

Sara Wearing a Bonnet and Coat

c. 1904/1906

Counterproof of a pastel, chine collé and reworked
0.729 × 0.581 m (28¾ × 22⅞ in.)
Rosenwald Collection 1980.45.9

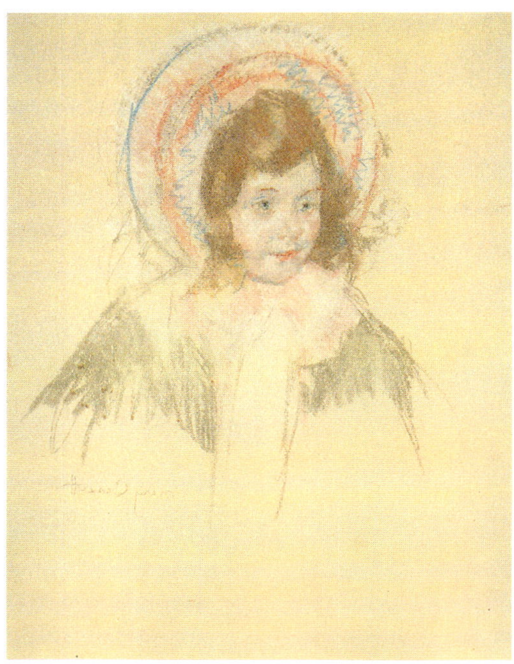

This pastel is related to numerous other works in all media—paintings, pastels, prints, and drawings—made by Cassatt during the early years of the twentieth century, whose subject, presented in a bust-level closeup, is an appealing little girl in an extravagant hat. The images of Margot, Simone, and this model, Sara, all three presumably recruited from the area near Cassatt's residence the Chateau Beaufresne in Mesnil-Théribus, appear again and again in similar poses.

There are, in fact, several works directly related to this one, a preparatory drawing in conté, a lithograph, and two other pastels. One of the pastels, like the lithograph, shows a slightly longer view of the child with a bow in her hair, and describes in much greater detail the volumes of her face and the intricate cape collar of her green coat. The present work seems to be a compromise between that work and the other pastel, which presents a shorter view of a bowless Sara, and does not articulate the details of her hat or model her face so fully. Together, these works give us insight into Cassatt's working method. In order to communicate the sense of spontaneous innocence achieved in her images of these children, the artist needed to engage in deliberate thought and planning, and to consider a variety of compositional alternatives.

If the prevalence of hats in these works has some meaning, it is certainly elusive. Cassatt often framed the faces of adult sitters with prominent headpieces, and she herself is known to have modeled for several of Degas' millinery scenes. Hats, with their bows, flowers, and streamers, are suggestive of the trappings of femininity. Visually, they add to the formal interest of Cassatt's work, as frames and foils for the heads they surround. They also must have provided her young sitters with a captivating diversion, the opportunity to play dress-up with the artist's collection of exotic props.

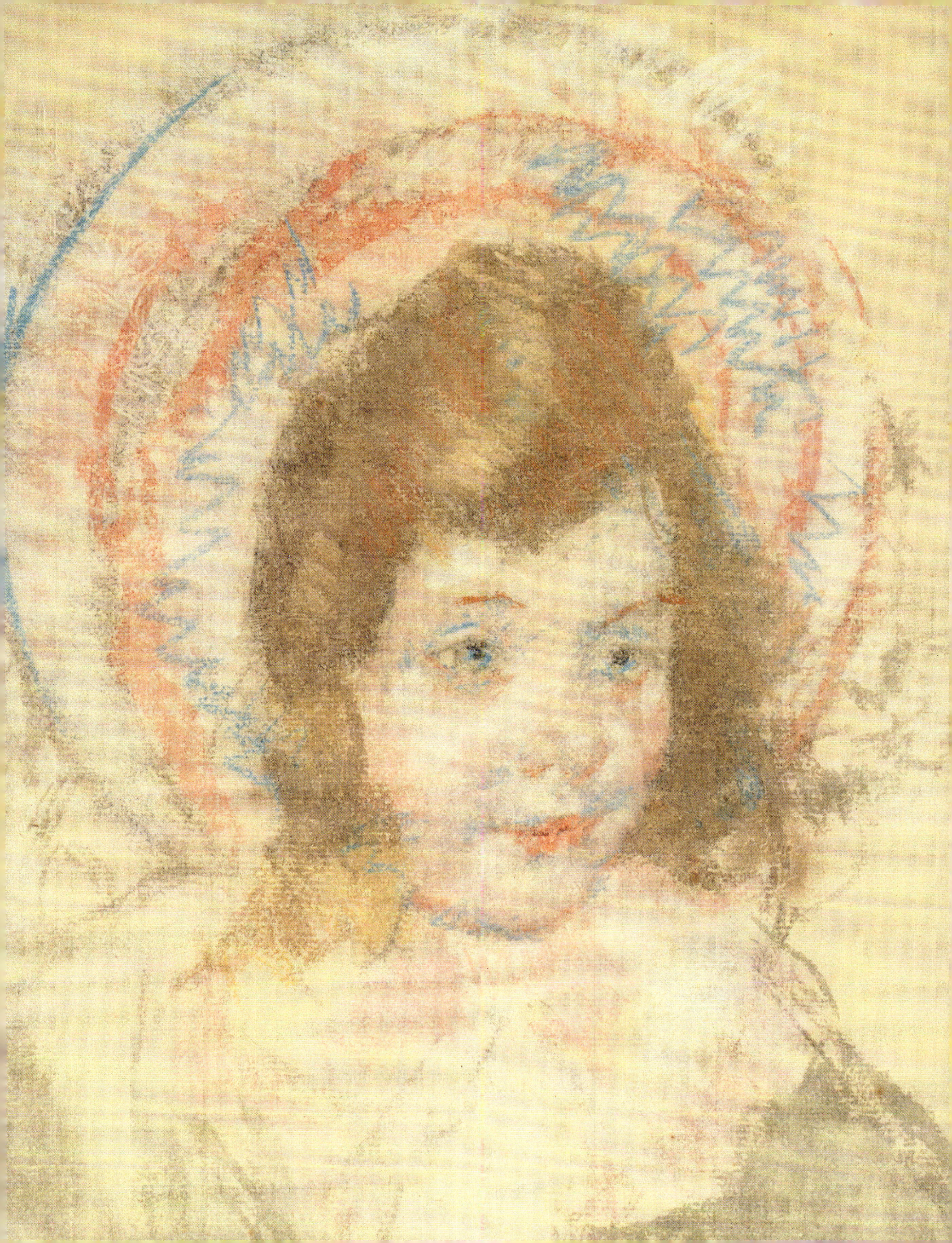

27

Mother and Child

c. 1905

Canvas
0.921 × 0.737 m (36¼ × 29 in.)
Chester Dale Collection 1963.10.98

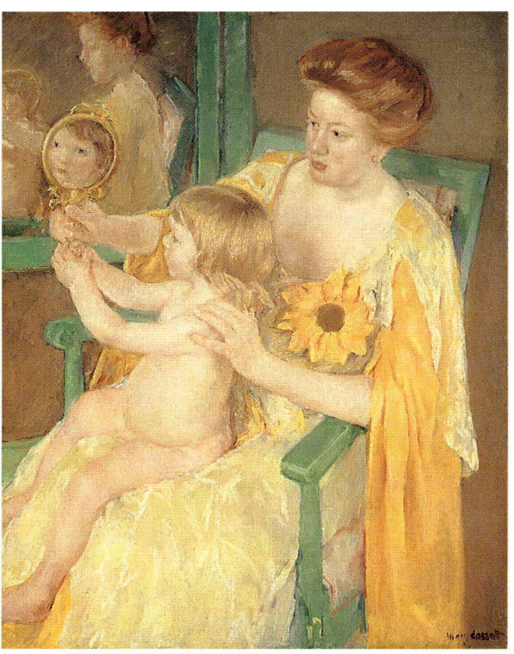

Cassatt in this work emphasizes the link between an elegantly attired mother and her naked daughter. A circular pattern dominates, connecting the woman and child to each other—and to the upheld mirror in which the child's face is reflected—through the rhythm of their arms and the placement of round forms. The giant sunflower on the mother's bodice, another important circle, serves to punctuate the movement from mother's head to daughter's. The gazes of both figures are focused on the same spot, the girl's reflection, a device frequently used by Cassatt to express her figures' unity. A pastel, *Mother Combing Her Child's Hair* (c. 1901), places the same figures in a similar setting, replete with green-edged chair and wall mirror, but lacks the focus of this work with its circular rhythm and unified gazes.

Although Cassatt probably did not intend the flower to be overtly symbolic, it contributes to the meaning of the work, suggesting youth and its flowering. Likewise, the mirrors also invite interpretation. The small one is of the type found in Renaissance paintings on the theme of Vanitas, in which a young woman gazing at her reflection is often contrasted with a hideous old crone. Cassatt treats the relationship between the generations of women with greater kindness; rather than highlighting youth's fleeting nature, the mother helps her daughter in her growth toward womanhood.

Yet Cassatt's point of view remains unclear. Some viewers suggest that she makes a negative comment concerning the social requirement that a free and unencumbered girl assume the trappings of femininity in order to become a proper lady. The contrast between the girl's nudity and the mother's sophisticated costume, the somewhat concerned look on the mother's face, and the multiple mirrors that perhaps underscore the importance of a woman knowing how she is seen are all details of the work that support this interpretation.

Stylistically, this work typifies Cassatt's later oeuvre, with its rich, almost brassy, use of color and significant emphasis on volumetric forms.

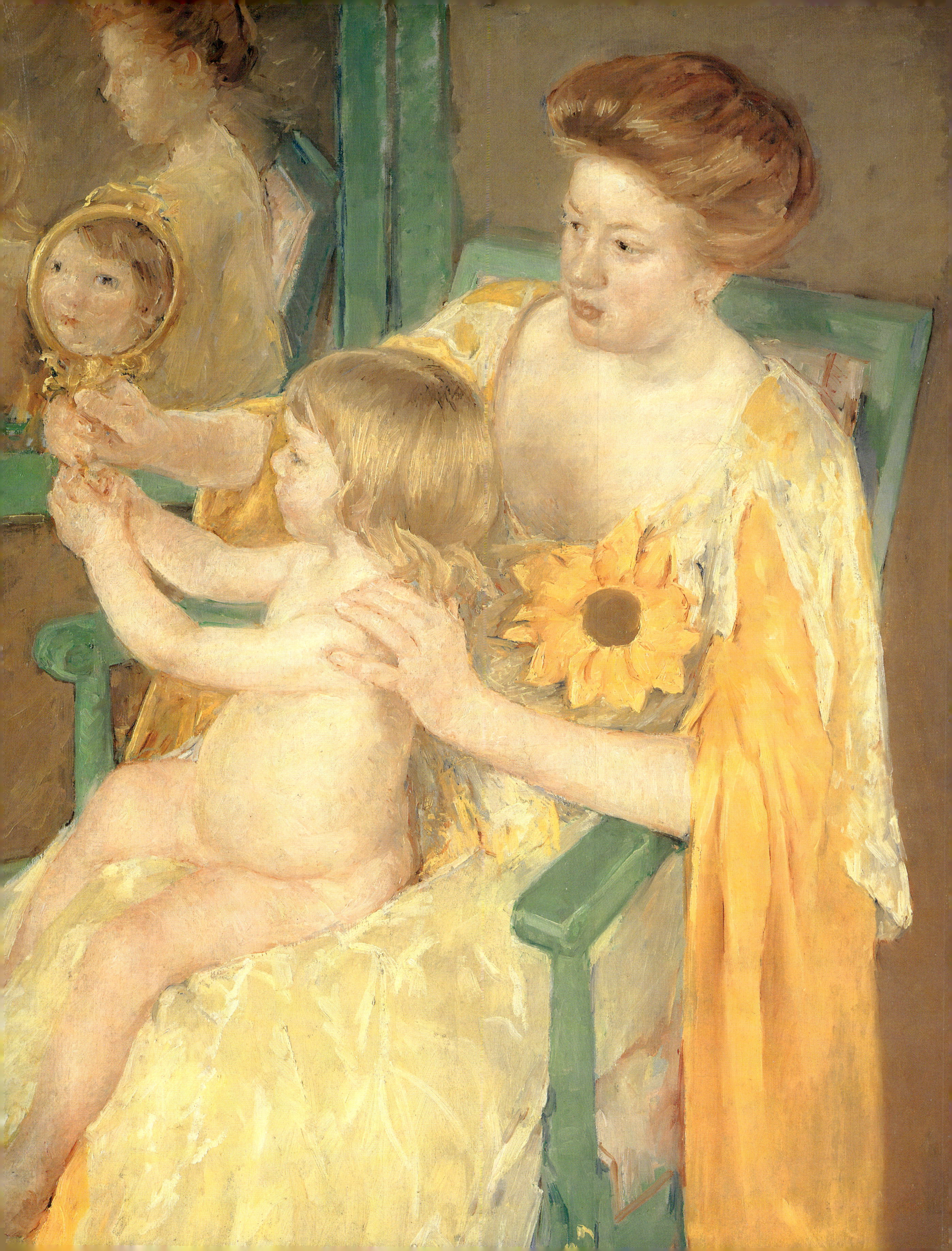

Selected Bibliography

Breeskin, Adelyn Dohme. *Mary Cassatt: A Catalogue Raisonné of the Graphic Work.* Reprint of *The Graphic Work of Mary Cassatt, a Catalogue Raisonné,* 1948. Washington, D.C.: Smithsonian Institution Press, 1979.

Breeskin, Adelyn Dohme. *Mary Cassatt: A Catalogue Raisonné of the Oils, Pastels, Watercolors, and Drawings.* Washington, D.C.: Smithsonian Institution Press, 1970.

Hale, Nancy. *Mary Cassatt, a Biography of the Great American Painter.* Garden City, N.Y.: Doubleday and Co., 1975.

Lindsay, Suzanne G. *Mary Cassatt and Philadelphia.* Philadelphia: Philadelphia Museum of Art, 1985.

Mathews, Nancy Mowll, ed. *Cassatt and Her Circle: Selected Letters.* New York: Abbeville Press, 1984.

Pollock, Griselda. *Mary Cassatt.* New York: Harper and Row, 1980.

Pollock, Griselda. *Vision and Difference: Femininity, Feminism and the Histories of Art.* London and New York: Routledge, 1988.

Segard, Achille. *Mary Cassatt: Un Peintre des enfants et des mères.* Paris: Librairie Paul Ollendorff, 1913.

Smith-Rosenberg, Carroll. "The Female World of Love and Ritual: Relations between Women in Nineteenth-Century America." In *Disorderly Conduct: Visions of Gender in Victorian America.* New York: Alfred A. Knopf, 1985.

Sweet, Frederick A. *Miss Mary Cassatt: Impressionist from Pennsylvania.* Norman, Okla.: University of Oklahama Press, 1966.

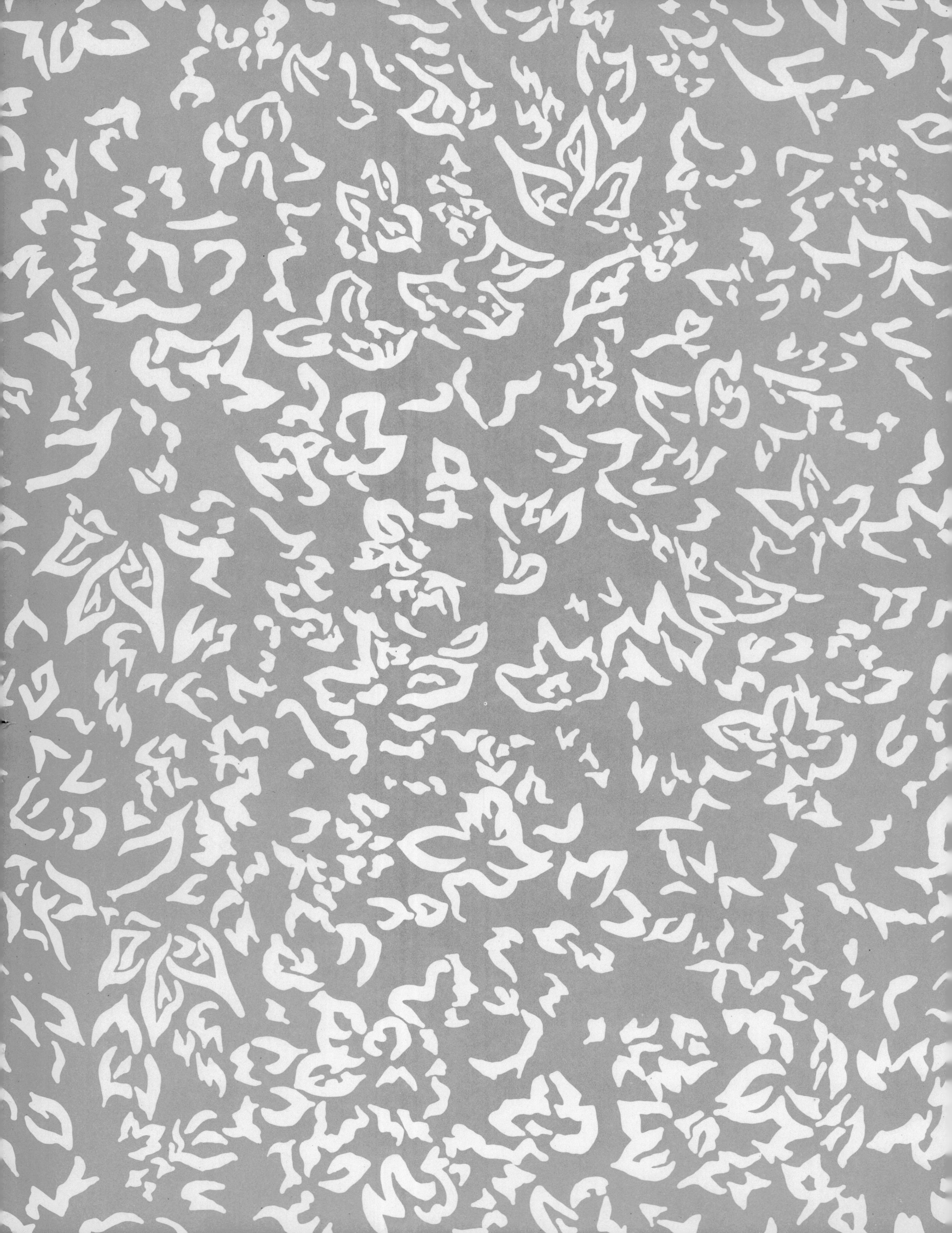